D1491932

SNUFF MILL on the RIVER FROME

(Near Stapleton)

BRISTOL: Drawn, Lithog.ᵈ & Pub.ᵈ by W.A.Frank   1831.

SNUFF
AND
SNUFF-BOXES

by

HUGH McCAUSLAND

'You abuse snuff! Perhaps it is the
final cause of the human nose.'

SAMUEL TAYLOR COLERIDGE

LONDON
THE BATCHWORTH PRESS

Published in 1951 by
BATCHWORTH PRESS LTD
54 Bloomsbury Street, London, W.C.1

Made and Printed in Great Britain by
GREYCAINES
(Taylor Garnett Evans & Co. Ltd.)
Watford, Herts.

Contents

Illustrations

Foreword

THE taking, making and selling of snuff in the British Isles, and the principal kinds of snuff-boxes used there, are the subjects chiefly considered in these pages. Less fully dealt with, and only in so far as they have seemed incidental to the story of snuffing in Britain, are associations of other countries with snuff and snuff-boxes. A little of the history of smoking and other uses of tobacco also has a place, as being—particularly in early days— inseparable from that of snuffing.

Grateful acknowledgments are made to a number of donors of information which has proved of great value in compiling this book, especially those parts of it that deal with the selling and manufacture of snuff. Historically interesting and snuffily invaluable old account books and trade records of the firm of Fribourg & Treyer, of Haymarket, London, have been freely and kindly placed at the Author's disposal by Mr R. H. Bridgman Evans. Mr S. E. West, of the same Snuff House, has given much time and trouble to the interpretation of manuscript records, the handwriting and meaning of which, when obscured by time, might have been unintelligible to anyone not possessed of his knowledge of the snuff trade of the past. Mr A. T. Law, of Messrs Gallaher, Ltd, Belfast and London, has provided lengthy and most helpful notes on certain aspects of snuff manufacture and distribution, in which he is a specialist. Much authoritative detail concerning snuff-making in the past as well as in the present has been supplied by Mr Albert Harland, of Messrs J. & H. Wilson, Limited, Westbrook Mill; and by Mr W. Wilson, of Messrs Wilson & Company, Sharrow Mills; both of Sheffield. And as kindly given have been the answers to questions addressed to managements or representatives of several other Houses, among them the long-established London retail businesses of Messrs John Hardham & Company, of Fleet Street; D. N. & S. Radford, of the same snuffy thoroughfare; and G. Smith & Sons, of Charing Cross Road.

Equal thanks are due to owners who have allowed prints, photographs and relics to be reproduced among the illustrations.

CHAPTER I

The Development of
Snuff-taking and Smoking

WHEN Columbus made his second voyage of discovery at the end of the fifteenth century he was accompanied by one Romano Pane, a Franciscan friar, who took note of the habits of the Indians of the New World. Outstanding among the novelties thus observed was the use of the herb later known as tobacco, which the Indians enjoyed in two distinct ways. One way was by burning the tobacco and inhaling its smoke; the other was by inhaling or sniffing the herb itself in a dust or powder form. Though these people used hollow canes, half a cubit[1] long, through which to take their dust, it consisted —like all true snuff, however much flavoured, scented or otherwise treated—of tobacco reduced to a powder.

Coupled in this early record, smoking and snuff-taking remained always closely linked, though the two habits began to follow separate roads when tobacco reached Europe. When once it had been introduced from the West, the use of tobacco spread rapidly; nation after nation took to snuffing or smoking. Most European countries adopted snuff in the first place and smoking later. In England smoking came first, to be succeeded by snuff-taking, a long and brilliant period of snuff's omnipresence giving place again to a general return of smoking. Earlier than in England snuff established itself in Ireland and Scotland; earlier still in France, where the fashion for taking snuff was set.

Jean Nicot, of Nîmes, who gave his name to the herb

---

[1] About 10 inches.

Nicotiana tabacum, and to nicotine, our everyday word for the poison content of tobacco, has been given the credit for having introduced the use of tobacco to Europe, and snuff was the form in which the tobacco of his procuring was first enjoyed. While in Portugal in 1559 as ambassador or accredited agent of the King of France, Nicot heard of the western herb of fabulous properties and set himself to the task of procuring a sample. Accounts vary as to how he provided himself with leaves and also, it appears, seeds of the tobacco which he sent home to France. One version of the story has it that he got them from a Dutch seaman; another tells of his finding tobacco plants in a flourishing state of growth in the garden in Lisbon of a certain Damian de Goes, a man of many interests of which botany was one. Of the tobacco leaves despatched by Nicot some were sent as a personal gift to Catherine de Medici, and these were accompanied by a description of the way in which the herb was enjoyed in the New World.

Following the methods of the Indians, Catherine is said to have had the leaves ground to a powder which she inhaled by means of a tube, and thus, rightly or wrongly, has taken her place in history as the first European snuff-taker of distinction. Medical practitioners, always anxious to supplement their very limited choice of drugs and remedies with anything that was novel, seized avidly on tobacco. The first of the physicians who were destined to exploit tobacco as a remedy for all manner of complaints in countless countries were those of the French Court. Unhesitatingly they pronounced tobacco to be a valuable medicine for diverse maladies and prescribed it in as many different forms as their ingenuity could suggest; to be taken inwardly in extracts, to be applied outwardly in poultices made of the leaves, or to be used in snuff form. Snuff even was specifically recommended to Charles IX, Catherine de Medici's son, as a palliative for headaches. Thus auspiciously launched on its career as a remedy, snuff was not long in proving itself a pleasant indulgence, and snuff-taking developed into a fashionable and eventually widespread habit.

The use of tobacco spread like wildfire over Europe and it was in the form of snuff, rather than as something to smoke or chew, that most Europeans elected to use tobacco. Medical advertisers of the new discovery were active all over the Continent endorsing the opinion of the French practitioners. Within six years of Nicot's introduction of tobacco to France a Spanish doctor, Nicolo Monardes of the university of Seville, had published a medical work largely devoted to advocating the use of tobacco for treating and curing widely differing complaints. Much circulated, and translated into several languages, one of which was English, this book did a great deal for tobacco in Europe.[1]

By the last quarter of the sixteenth century tobacco was known and used in one or other of its forms in all the countries of the world, not excepting those of the Far East. The next century saw the people of Europe carrying their passion for tobacco to such lengths that two Popes of Rome thought it necessary to issue solemn decrees at different periods banning both smoking and snuffing in church and making those who were guilty of such offences subject to excommunication. In the first of these Papal Bulls it was proclaimed that:

> . . . information has lately reached Us from the Dean and Chapter of the metropolitan church of Seville that in these parts the use of the herb commonly called tobacco has gained so strong a hold on persons of both sexes, yea even priests and clerics, that, We blush to state, during the actual celebration of Holy Mass they do not shrink from taking tobacco through the mouth or nostrils, thus soiling the altar linen and infecting the churches with its noxious fumes, sacrilegiously and to the great scandal of the pious.

[1] *Historia Medicinal de las Cosas de Nuestras Indias Occidentales* (Seville, 1574); first complete English edition, 1596.

The pronunciamento went on to

Prohibit and Interdict all persons of either sex, clergy or laity collectively and individually, from using snuff or tobacco in any form whatever in the churches in the diocese of Seville, their vestibules, vestries or immediate surroundings. All persons thus offending shall be punished by immediate excommunication, *ipso facto*, without further ado, in accordance with the present interdict.

Snuff again was mentioned in the second pronouncement, the work of a later Pope, which was couched in similarly strong terms and directed particularly against people who had been taking snuff or otherwise consuming tobacco within the walls of St. Peter's at Rome.

From all over the Continent at this period came news of the various attitudes adopted by kings and governments toward their subjects' ever increasing use of tobacco. Less was heard of the virtues of the herb as a medicine and a beneficial influence, and more of its baneful qualities as a drug and of its insidiousness as a vice. A somewhat contradictory compromise was reached by the Emperor of Austria, who, while condemning tobacco as injuring the health, shortening life, depleting the financial resources of the country and being the cause of many fires, yet admitted its value as a medicine and therefore permitted it to be sold, but only by chemists and apothecaries.

Elsewhere on every hand the demand for tobacco was made a valuable source of state revenue. Taxes on importation were levied and then increased, and monopolies were granted to privileged importers or were retained by kings or ruling powers as too lucrative to be parted with on any terms. In Venice, then an independent republic, a tobacco tax was introduced at an early date and later was followed by a monopoly. In France, when Louis XIII was on the throne and the control of the nation's affairs was mainly in the hands of Cardinal

Richelieu, who was an objector to smoking and the fashionable habit of snuffing, a tobacco tax was in force before the year 1630. Some forty-five years later a monopoly was introduced, and excused on the grounds that it would provide funds for war expenses, by Louis XIV, who professed to loathe tobacco in any form.

Snuff came later to England than to the Continent. Its use by the English followed a long period in which smoking had become a widespread national habit indulged in to excess by every class and degree of the population. Queen Elizabeth's reign saw tobacco introduced, either by Sir John Hawkins in 1565 or by Sir Walter Raleigh and Sir Francis Drake at a somewhat later date. History records more than one version of the first part of tobacco's story in this country and is as uncertain about the year in which the smoking craze began as of the man responsible for it; tradition, however, accords the credit or blame to Raleigh rather than to his associates. That Raleigh set an early example in smoking is a belief commemorated in several such legends as the one telling of his servant's introduction to tobacco. During his hours of writing and study, the story has it, Raleigh called to his servant to bring him a jug of beer; his pipe was lit and smoke was pouring from his mouth and nostrils when the man obeyed the order. Horrified and convinced that an excess of study had set his master's brains on fire, he did his best to 'extinguish' the conflagration by dashing the generous quart of small beer in Raleigh's face. It was Raleigh who organised the settlement of English colonists in Virginia—where later they grew some of the finest smoking tobacco—by sending expeditions there in 1585 and 1587. His name remains coupled with tobacco until literally the last day of his life, when, it is said, 'he took two pipes' during his final hours before going to the scaffold.

Of unestablished origin are some old lines associating Hawkins with tobacco and giving snuffing an equal place with smoking and chewing:

> Up comes brave Hawkins on the beach,
> 'Shiver my hull', he cries,
> 'What's these here games, my men?
> Why blame my eyes!
> Here's one as chews and one as snuffs,
> And t'other of the three
> Is a'smoking like a chimney,
> They've found out Tobackee!'

The same obscurity clouds the origin of the word tobacco, generally thought to have been acquired from the West Indian island of Tobago which was discovered by Columbus in 1498; other possible sources of the name are Tabacco and Tobasca.

For long after Hawkins' and Raleigh's time tobacco history in England is concerned mainly with the people's wholesale adoption of smoking, more than equalling any national passion for tobacco seen abroad, and with various attempts to check the spread of the habit. When the seventeenth century opened, women as well as men had taken to smoking; before long children were being taught how to smoke by their elders and were given pipes when they were hungry to save the cost or trouble of giving them food. The first accomplishment of youths of good family was to master the use of a pipe, and the cheapness of tobacco recommended it to the poorest and humblest of the people. Smoking houses, where pipes and tobacco were provided for patrons, were as common in London and other cities as beer houses and taverns. In the latter smoking accompanied drinking and was the normal sequel to a meal in the manner noted by Stow:

> It was now evening and supper time. My guide led me to the Tavern called the Rose, in the Poultry. . . . Here there was music, and the drawers ran about with supper and wine. A capon

with a flask of Malmsey warmed the heart of my old guide. After supper we took tobacco and more wine, while boys sang Madrigals very sweetly.

Paul Hentzner, a German who visited London in 1598, patronized the popular sports of bull and bear baiting and found:

> At these spectacles, and everywhere else, the English are con-
> stantly seen smoking the Nicotean weed, which in America is
> called Tobaca, and generally in this manner; they have pipes on
> purpose made of clay, into the further end of which they put the
> herb, so dry that it may be rubbed into powder, and lighting it
> they draw the smoke into their mouths, which they puff out
> again through their nostrils, along with plenty of phlegm and
> defluction from the head.[1]

Londoners were spending no less a sum than £300,000 a year on tobacco at this time. The figure, given by that painstaking London historian, Sir Walter Besant, is more revealing than words when accompanied by the statement that tobacco was commonly sold in pennyworths. For twopence enough tobacco could be bought to fill a man's pocket, and London boasted no fewer than seven thousand vendors of tobacco, including, no doubt, the many apothecaries who found it a lucrative part of their business. In summing up the extent of the smoking craze the same authority is eloquent:

> During this time the use of tobacco penetrated all ranks and
> classes of society. The grave divine, the soldier, the lawyer, the
> gallant about town, the merchant, the craftsman, the 'prentice,
> all used pipes. At the theatre the young fellow called for his pipe
> and for tobacco and began to smoke; presently he rose and,
> walking over to the boxes, presented his pipe to any lady of his
> acquaintance.
> People went to bed with tobacco box and pipe and candle on a
> table by the bedside in case they might wake up in the night and
> feel inclined for tobacco. After supper in a middle-class family,

---

[1] *Travels in England during the Reign of Queen Elizabeth*, edited and translated by Horace Walpole, 1797.

all the men and women smoked together. Nay, it is even stated that the very children in school took a pipe of tobacco instead of breakfast, the master smoking with them and instructing them how to bring the smoke through the nostrils in the fashion of the day. . . . Every man carried a tobacco box, steel and touch. . . .

There was perhaps good enough reason for James I to object to a vice that had so enslaved his people by the time he came to the throne in 1603. Objection, however, is altogether too mild a word to describe the King's feeling, which amounted to a personal hatred of tobacco that was to become almost a fanatical obsession. Losing little time in proving himself the most relentless as well as the most powerful of tobacco's enemies, he brought all his considerable powers of penmanship and invective to the support of taxation in a campaign against smoking. A tobacco tax of 6s. 8d. on the pound, one of the first fiscal measures of King James's reign, was introduced in 1604, with the declaration that:

> Whereas tobacco being of late years found out and brought from foreign parts in small quantities, was taken and used by the better sort, both then and now, only as a physic, to preserve health, but is now, at this day, through evil custom and the toleration thereof, excessively taken by a number of riotous and disorderly persons of mean and base condition, who do spend most of their time in that idle vanity to the evil example and corrupting of others; and also do consume the wages which many of them get by their labour, not caring at what price they buy that drug; by which immoderate taking of tobacco the health of a great number of our people is impaired and their bodies weakened and made unfit for labour; besides that also a great part of the treasure of our land is spent and exhausted by this only drug, so licentiously abused by the meaner sort; all which enormous inconvenience we do perceive to proceed principally from the great quantity of tobacco brought into this our realm, which excess might in great part be restricted by some good imposition to be laid upon it.

A Counterblaste To Tobacco, written by King James himself and published in 1604, remains after three and a half centuries unsurpassed in the literature of would-be reformers and crusaders against vice. Only the inspiration of loathing could provide such terms as the King used to describe smoking. Among them we find: 'A custome lothesome to the eye, hatefull to the nose, harmfull to the braine, dangerous to the lungs, and in the black stinking fume thereof nearest resembling the horrible Stigian smoke of the Pit that is bottomlesse. . . . This filthie noveltie, a great vanitie and uncleannesse . . . a great contempt of God's good giftes'. Deploring that tobacco's 'publicke use, at all times, in all places, hath now so far prevailed, as diverse men very sound both in judgment and complexion have bene at last forced to take it without desire', for no better reason than a fear of being thought singular, the King had words as strong for those who 'Sit tossing of Tobacco pipes, and puffing of the smoke of Tobacco one to another, making the filthie smoke and stink thereof to exhale athwart the dishes and infect the aire'. Even, he found, were such men as 'cannot welcome a friend now, but straight they must bee in hand with Tobacco . . . moreover, which is a great iniquitie and against all humanitie, the husband shall not bee ashamed to reduce thereby his delicate, wholesome and cleane complexioned wife to that extremitie that either shee must also corrupt her sweet breathe therewith, or else resolve to live in a perpetual stinking torment'.

In his battle against tobacco James had the support of many men of influence in the country. They included courtiers, writers and physicians, some of them sincere enough in their belief that smoking was a harmful habit, others mere seekers of the royal favour. It says much for the strength of the hold tobacco had taken on the nation that all the powerful attacks made upon its use were survived. As we have seen illustrated again in recent times, increased cost of tobacco due to taxation

B

deterred smokers so little that their numbers increased rather than decreased. King James would have stopped the growing of tobacco in Virginia altogether if he had been able to; as it was he issued a proclamation in the colony in 1619 limiting the production of each planter to one hundredweight per annum, endeavouring to divert the activities of the colonists to the production of corn, potash and livestock and to the cultivation of silkworms. The effect of this measure, however, was so harmful to the rising colony that five years later the King substituted an order forbidding the importation of tobacco to England except from Virginia and the Somers Islands, thereby giving the colonists a virtual monopoly. It remained for Charles I in later years to confirm the sale of tobacco a royal monopoly and to prohibit his colonies from selling to any other state an output which he took for Britain at a price of his own fixing.

Meanwhile in England King James kept up his attempts to curb the people's smoking with but little hope of success. It is said that but once in his lifelong campaign against tobacco did he make a personal concession to its virtues; and that once was in a pigsty. Out hunting one day in desolate country, he was forced by a torrent of rain to take shelter under the only available roof, that of a sty from which the normal occupants were hurriedly driven to make way for the King. After enduring the natural fragrance of the place for some while, he 'caused a pipeful to be taken' by a companion; thus proving the truth of a statement made by Howell —the original teller of this tale—that tobacco smoke 'is one of the wholesomest scents that is against all contagious Airs, for it overmasters all other smells'.

A visit made by King James to Cambridge gave rise to an early mention of the use of snuff in England; the University authorities, making preparation for the King's sojourn in the town and bearing in mind his particular dislike of tobacco, proclaimed a temporary ban on the use of tobacco by undergraduates or college servants, the same to cover the taking of snuff in church or college.

Though the great age of snuff-taking in England began in earnest only with the eighteenth century and direct references to Englishmen practising the habit in the seventeenth century are not numerous, it is clear that young men of fashion were gradually seeking an alternative to smoking. The very excess to which smoking had been carried by the lower orders provided a reason for what W. A. Penn has called the 'Bloods of the seventeenth century' to introduce a new and less common custom. The remaining alternatives were few. The enjoyment of tobacco by chewing it could be left to mariners and other manual workers sufficiently tough of fibre to be able to assimilate the juice as a beverage. Other methods of taking the herb were as unsuited to the taste of men of culture as that mentioned in one of James Howell's *Familiar Letters* (1645–50):[1]

> In Barbary and other parts of Africk, it is wonderful what a small pill of Tobacco will do; for those who used to ride post through the sandy Deserts, where they meet not with anything that's potable or edible, sometimes three Dayes together, they use to carry small Balls or Pills of Tobacco, which being under the Tongue, it affords them a perpetual Moisture, and takes off the Appetite for some days.

There remained snuff-taking, the elegant habit already so fashionable among men of polish and refinement on the Continent. Its adoption in England was only a question of time. As a habit it had an English precedent in the sniffing of aromatic or sneezing powders probably made from home-grown herbs. Probably during the plague

---

[1] An ardent Royalist, Howell was imprisoned for his beliefs from 1643 to 1651; while confined in the Fleet during this time he wrote his *Familiar Letters*, addressed to imaginary correspondents and containing many enlightening notes on contemporary life.

of 1614—when physicians again were busy recommending tobacco as a prophylactic—snuff was found more agreeable than smoke to many people. Certainly snuff had found advocates in fair numbers by the time of the greater plague of 1665, for before this the pinch of snuff, taken for pleasure rather than for any supposed good effects, had become an indulgence with some of the Roundheads, though Cromwell himself was neither a tobacco addict nor an admirer of those who were. Butler speaks of snuff-taking in the Cromwellian period, one passage in *Hudibras* reading, 'After h'had ministred a Dose of Snuff-Mundungus to his Nose'.

In Ireland snuff was taken in great quantities, mainly by the peasant class, long before it was widely used in England, and evidence of its popularity with both men and women in mid-seventeenth century is supplied by James Howell. Part of a passage on tobacco tells of the Irish use of 'smutchin' and the method of taking it:

> The Spaniards and the Irish take it [tobacco] most in powder or smutchin, and it mightily refreshes the Brain, and I believe there is as much taken this way in Ireland as there is in Pipes in England; one shall commonly see the serving-maid upon the washing-block, and the swain upon the plough-share, when they are tired with Labour, take out their boxes of Smutchin, and draw it into their nostrils with a Quill, and it will beget new spirits in them, with a fresh Vigor to fall to their Work again.

The taking of a pinch of snuff in these early days entailed a preparatory ritual almost as elaborate as that of the present day smoker of cigarettes of his own rolling, who carries a rolling-machine, cigarette-papers and loose tobacco and spends nearly as much time in preparing something to smoke as he does in consuming it. To a later age belonged the delicate pinch of snuff taken elegantly between forefinger and thumb from a box which might be a little work of art, and which had been freshly filled with any one of scores of varieties, strengths and substances of plain or scented snuffs supplied by snuffman or blender. The pioneer snuff-taker of the seventeenth and early eighteenth centuries bought his snuff in the solid form of what was known as a *carotte*, a roll or twist of hard tobacco; this he ground to powder as he needed it. Snuff-boxes were carried which were fitted with a grater like a small file on which the *carotte* was rubbed to produce a coarse snuff. Some of these snuff-grater boxes still survive, the better ones being made of silver or ivory and having separate compartments for a section of *carotte* and for the powder ground from it. Later English varieties of snuff, of the coarser ground kind most nearly resembling that which was hand rasped from the *carotte*, were to be known as Rappee from the French *raper* (to grate). When snuff had been prepared in advance, it was commonly carried in a box fitted with a quill which was used to sniff through in the manner of the New World Indians and of Catherine de Medici. The more elaborate of quill-boxes were provided with a spring controlling the amount of snuff emitted at each sniff.

The people of Scotland, like those of Ireland, were ahead of the English in adopting the snuff habit. In the eighteenth century the Scot's unbounded addiction to snuff was to become a byword in England and was to lead to the general use of effigies of Highlanders as signs outside snuff-sellers' shops; the seventeenth century, however, saw Scotland a country of confirmed snuffers when but few were to be found south of the Border. 'With durk, and snap-work and snuff-mill' is a line occuring in Cleland's Poems of 1689, an early reference to the mill or mull of horn commonly used in Scotland in place of a snuff-box. The literature of a little later date bristles with allusions to the Gaelic interpretations of the word snuff—the *snishon*, *sneishing* and similar equivalents of the Irishman's *smutchin*, and Scotch snuff emerges as a tobacco preparation with a distinction and character of its own. Nose shovels, used to raise snuff from the mull to the nostrils, were a part of Scottish snuffing ritual at an early date and suggest the quantities absorbed.

The suggestion is made in Penn's *The Soverane Herb* (1901) that it was the cheapness of snuff, as compared to smoking tobacco, which made it so popular with the thrifty Scot. Notwithstanding this opinion it seems reasonable to assume that snuffing crept into Scotland as it did into so many other countries, as a fashion backed in the first place by medical recommendation. Once begun, the habit—like all pleasantly insidious habits—of taking the 'pungent grains of titillating dust' acquired its own attraction and mastery. Men and women fell victims to snuff as easily as in after generations they did to the cigarette habit, progressing gradually from the first sneezing stage of initiation to the final status of a hardened, habitual snuffer to whom a sneeze is a thing unknown. The graduation of a snuff-taker has been well described in Hone's *Table Book* (1827) by one who found that 'the office grew out of my liking a pinch now and then, and carrying a bit of snuff, screwed up in paper, wherewith, some two or three times a day I delighted to treat myself to a sensation and a sneeze'; thereafter he 'resorted on all difficult occasions to a pinch of snuff' for inspiration or comfort; and eventually pronounced, 'my prime minister of pleasure is my snuff-box . . . as soon as I wear out one snuff-box I get another'.

In a country so obsessed with smoking as was seventeenth century England the adoption of snuff was hardly noticeable. That smoking was soon to be displaced by a general passion for snuff-taking seemed as improbable then as it seems remarkable now, when snuff users again are, and long have been, a minority in a nation of smokers. Chronicles of the second half of the seventeenth century make it clear that tobacco's hold on the people was as strong, or even stronger, than in the first half, but the references to tobacco are nearly all to its use in pipes, seldom to snuff.

Detractors and critics were active, as always in the history of tobacco. Two or three years before the Fire of London Sir William Davenant wrote:

> I see it [smoking] grows so much in fashion that methinks your children begin to play with broken pipes instead of corals, to make way for their teeth.

To this he added a statement of his personal feelings:

> You know my aversion to a certain weed that governs amongst your coarser acquaintance as much as lavender amongst your coarser linen; to which, in my apprehension, your sea-coal smoke seems a very Portugal perfume.

More frequently expressed was the opposite and popular view, never perhaps more forcefully championed than by the entertaining James Howell writing in his *Letters:*

> To usher in again old Janus, I send you a parcel of Indian perfume, which the Spaniards call the Holy herb, in regard of various virtues it hath; but we call it Tobacco. If moderately and reasonably taken 'tis good for many Things; it helps Digestion, taken awhile after meat; a leaf or two being steeped o'er Night in a little White-wine is a Vomit that never fails in its Operations; it is a good companion to one that converseth with dead Men; for if one hath been poring too long upon a book, or is toil'd with the Pen, and stupfy'd with Study, it quickeneth him and dispels those Clouds that usually o'erset the Brain. . . . It cannot endure a Spider or a Flea with such like Vermin, and if your Hawk be troubled with any such being blown into his feathers, it frees him; it is good to fortify and preserve the sight, the smoke being let in round about the Balls of the Eyes once a week, and frees them from all rheums, driving them back by way of Repercussion: being taken backward 'tis excellent good against the Cholic, and taken into the Stomach, it will heat and cleanse it; for I could instance in a great Lord (my Lord of Sunderland, Presi-

dent of York) who told me that he, taking it downward into his Stomach, it made him cast up an Imposthume, Bag and all, which had been a long time engendering out of a bruise he had received at Foot-ball, and so preserved his life for many years.

Now to descend from the substance of the smoke to the ashes, 'tis well known that the medicinal virtues thereof are very many; but they are so common that I will spare the insertion of them here; but if one would try a pretty conclusion how much smoke there is in a pound of Tobacco, the Ashes will tell him: for let a pound be exactly weighed, and the ashes kept charily and weighed afterwards, what wants of a Pound weight in the Ashes cannot be deny'd to have been smoke, which evaporated in the Air. I have been told that Sir Walter Raleigh won a Wager of Queen Elizabeth upon this Nicety.

Snuff, though but little used throughout England as a whole, was gaining advocates in London toward the end of the century. In coffee-houses, which a little later were to be associated so much with fashionable snuff-taking, snuff-boxes were making an appearance. The poet Dryden, already a confirmed snuffer, was often to be seen in a London coffee-house receiving the homage of younger literary men and occasionally paying one of them the compliment of offering him a pinch from his snuff-box. London also boasted a few snuff shops, fore-runners of many to come. A certain James Norcock was advertising in the *London Gazette* as early as in 1683 to the effect that 'all sorts of Snuffs, Spanish and Italian' could be obtained from him; evidently the importation of foreign snuffs, later to reach England in countless varieties and enormous quantities, had begun. Norcock also claimed to be a 'Snuffmaker and Perfumer', which suggests an early acquaintance with imparting perfume flavours to snuff. Slight as they were, these things were symptoms of the coming prevalence of snuff-taking.

CHAPTER II

Snuff-taking in the Eighteenth Century

THE eighteenth century was, so far as Britain was concerned, a century of snuff-taking. Smoking became practically eclipsed by the cult of snuff which spread, as the century advanced, to men and women of all conditions just as smoking had done in earlier years. Even the foreigners who helped the English to acquire the habit were moved to comment in astonished terms on the enormous amount of snuff consumed in eighteenth century Britain.

In England snuff made rapid progress from the opening of the century, the first three years seeing the limited numbers of the snuff-takers of the previous century many times multiplied and the habit well on the way to becoming as general a one as it already was in Ireland and Scotland. French manners and fashions were being widely followed in England when Queen Anne came to the throne in 1702, notwithstanding the nearly continuous state of war which for so long had existed between the two countries, and the conditions and contacts of war themselves did much toward promoting English snuff-taking. Men returning from the Continent brought snuff with them and introduced it to their families and friends; prisoners of war were snuff-takers; and snuff in bulk even had a prominent place among the captured prizes of war.

Admiral Sir George Rooke unintentionally caused snuff to be introduced and distributed on a wholesale scale in southern England in 1702, two years before he and Sir Cloudesley Shovel captured Gibraltar. In com-

mand of a British fleet making a raid on Port St. Mary,
he captured and destroyed certain French ships of war
and Spanish treasure ships in Vigo Bay. Among the
spoils taken from the Spanish vessels were many
hundreds of casks filled with a brown powder which
subsequently was identified as fine snuff imported from
Havana. Fifty tons of this snuff were distributed among
Rooke's seamen, each man being left to dispose of his
perquisite on the best terms he could obtain by retailing
it at home. For some while thereafter sea ports round
the southern coast of England were flooded with snuff,
threepence or fourpence a pound being about the price
commanded by this first large-scale importation of snuff
in a prepared state.

So large a quantity distributed at so low a price certainly advertised snuff as it had never yet been advertised
in England, making snuff-takers of thousands of people
hitherto ignorant of its charms, and the crews of Sir
George Rooke's ships of war have been remembered as
wholesale snuff salesmen by most historians allowing any
space at all to the origins of a habit which was soon to
become a national one. Apart from noting this incident
and its far-reaching effects, however, contemporary
chroniclers are singularly uncommunicative on the
subject of snuff indulgence, treating it rather as a thing
too generally practised to be noticed at any length and,
while no doubt using snuff themselves in quantities
sufficient to stimulate their ideas on weightier matters,
leaving to a few specialists the task of recording snuff's
early history in England.

One of the writers whose interest in the subject was
particular and personal produced a treatise in the first
years of the rise of snuff from comparative obscurity to
wide popularity in England, and is helpful historically
in giving 1702 as the year in which the snuffing habit
became generally noticeable. The work deals mainly

with the scenting and preparation of snuff; for the rest it rather dismisses those who took snuff in England before this time as a negligible number of men who had learnt the habit abroad or were themselves foreigners, and is a little forgetful of the English addicts of Dryden's generation, to say nothing of Irish and Scottish precedents.

Himself a foreigner living in London, the author of this work was a quaint and amusing character with a place of his own in snuff history. By name Charles Lillie, he was by trade a perfumer who had left France with the idea of helping fashionable London society to a better understanding of the mysteries of scents and essences in general, and in particular the imparting of perfume flavours to snuff. His knowledge of these things he exploited to his own considerable gain, becoming well known as 'The French Perfumer' while residing at the corner of Beaufort Buildings in the Strand, where Henry Fielding also spent a part of his life. Apart from his activities as a perfumer, Lillie dabbled in journalism and was the secretary of 'Mr. Bickerstaff's Court of Honour' which, held in Shire Lane, was one of the diversions of the lighter-hearted members of society, and the scene of such trials as those remembered by Leigh Hunt: 'where people had actions brought against them for pulling out their watches while their superiors were talking; and for brushing feathers off a gentleman's coat with a cane "value fivepence" '. Dean Swift, who early in the eighteenth century made use of the pseudonym 'Isaac Bickerstaff', was, it seems, one of several distinguished men of letters who patronized and encouraged the versatile Monsieur Lillie, another who did so having been Sir Richard Steele, the founder of the *Tatler* (1709), in which were printed a number of Lillie's writings. Lillie also published in 1725 two volumes made up of contributions rejected by the *Tatler*, and

the subject in later years of an acid comment made
by Leigh Hunt in *The Town*: 'We believe they had no
merit'.

Lillie and other men coming from snuff-taking
countries did much toward promoting the habit in
England, but yet more influential advocates were forth-
coming in the shape of medical practitioners, both
genuine and quack. Growing every day in popularity,
snuff was soon to be as widely recommended for curing
or alleviating various common complaints as tobacco
had been in the past, and as snuff itself had been in other
countries. No important town physician went about his
work without the support of his snuff-box or entered an
infected dwelling without helping himself liberally to
snuff as a preventive measure; his patients were advised
to take it as a remedy for nasal and pulmonary troubles,
as well as for many other distempers for which it seemed
even less likely to prove effective. Humbler apothecaries
made a good thing of becoming snuff-sellers, and were
loud in its praises. Most market places and fair grounds
boasted their quack practitioners selling snuffs for which
unique properties were claimed, and the charges were
made accordingly.

The last-named type of snuff-seller had a great following early in the eighteenth century, and was endowed
with a power of convincing the credulous as great as
that of any cheap-jack of more recent times. Beyond the
ranks of itinerant and market place quacks who exploited
snuff were others of a superior order who carried on
business from London addresses, selling their wares by
advertisement. The terms in which they advertised were
as impressive as the prices that in some cases they were
able to obtain for allegedly imported snuffs, which,
whatever their origin, were probably much adulterated
with all kinds of harmful ingredients, the use of which
was to be made illegal by laws governing the sale of snuff

and tobacco in later years. Remembered by C. J. S. Thompson, in his book on the *Quacks of Old London* (1928), are several of these dealers in snuff to suit all pockets and nearly all common ailments. A Mr Harrison, whose headquarters were at the western end of the Royal Exchange, charged 6*s.* an ounce for his cheapest Lisbon snuff, and as much as 23*s.* for an ounce of his best, strongly recommending the latter for the improvement of the eyesight. Elsewhere 'Tongear',[1] German and Italian snuffs which were considered most efficacious in cases of toothache, cost only from one to two shillings the ounce. One of the first quacks to exploit snuff medicinally was one Edwyn Salter who did business at the house next door to the sign of the Sugar Loaf in Nevill's Alley, Fetter Lane, his speciality being a 'Sternutatory Snuff to fortify the brain and its animal faculties'. A bill dated in the year 1706 shows a charge of no more than 5*s.* a pound for Havana, Spanish and Seville snuffs referred to as the best, and advocated as 'a present remedy for the most violentest Headache or Toothache, infallible curers of Coughs or Ptsicks, and a preventive of those distempers'.

Between 23*s.* an ounce for one snuff and 5*s.* a pound for another is a disparity which seems capable of only one explanation, however beneficial Mr Harrison's best Lisbon may have been to the eyes, and clearly snuff of alleged superiority was exploited at the expense of the credulous in days before the establishment or recognition of the reputable snuff-sellers who began to appear later in the century. Mixtures of tobacco with rubbishy and even dangerous substances were quite commonly sold as snuff by unscrupulous traders of Queen Anne's time; the bulk of a shipment of foreign snuff could be doubled by mixing it with coloured earth or ground leaves from common trees, and any loss of pungency or

[1] Possibly so-called from the tonka or tonquin bean used to perfume snuffs

titillating qualities could be made up with touchwood, pepper or mineral acids, while if occasionally a snuff-taker died of lead poisoning it was nobody's business to suggest that he had been inhaling a powder coloured with umber, ochre or some other ingredient of paint. The wisest snuff-takers of this period no doubt were those who adhered to the practice of grinding their own snuff from the *carotte*, which, though not entirely above suspicion, was less likely to be harmfully adulterated than a prepared powder.

The names of most of the snuffs mentioned in the advertisements of the old quacks, however, do suggest, if they are to be believed, that foreign snuffs were being imported in considerable quantities. Throughout the century these imports were to increase, and as long as snuffing remained a fashionable habit most of the snuff taken in England, and nearly all that was preferred by the wealthier classes, was to be of foreign making. Always, too, the word snuff denoted a tobacco product, in early days often much adulterated and at any period subject to the addition of flavouring agents, but still basically tobacco. Claims of medicinal properties in snuffs of the eighteenth century carried no such implication as that of modern times, when medicinal powders without tobacco content are often recommended for the treatment of catarrh or colds under the courtesy title of 'snuff'. As all true wine is the product of the grape— notwithstanding the claims to wineship of the extracts of ginger and the gooseberry, so is all true snuff the product of tobacco and unrelated to the powdered sternutatories of the chemist's shop.

As the fashion for taking snuff gained ground, much less was heard of medical reasons for its use. Such excuses as that snuff was good for the eyes or the lungs became superfluous as the snuff-box took its place as an essential part of the equipment of every man of social standing and the practised handling of his box, with the exaggerated mannerisms accompanying the offering or taking of a pinch from it, were accepted as among the accomplishments of gentility. So rapidly did the snuff habit conquer English society that within the first half of Queen Anne's reign tobacco came to have little meaning, so far as the *beau-monde* was concerned, beyond snuff. To smoke had become a mark of vulgarity; only the lower orders—whose adoption of snuff was yet to follow—and certain country squires, soldiers and seamen remained entirely faithful to their pipes. Smoking was altogether taboo among those who frequented Court and the haunts of fashion, while snuff was taken in ever-increasing quantities as enthusiastically by women as by men. So it was, too, in the realms of wit and learning, of literature and art. In the coffee- and chocolate-houses that developed into so important a feature of eighteenth century town life as the meeting places of leading citizens, men who smoked made up but an insignificant minority among the many whose snuff-boxes were continually opening and closing.

Growing up together the snuff habit and the coffee-house habit were closely associated, both of them assuming immense importance in the social life of the century, both claiming among their devotees nearly every outstanding or entertaining figure of a picturesque age, and in the chronicles of London's coffee-houses much of the story of fashionable snuffing is to be found. As clubs were used later, men then used their coffee-houses, as places of meeting, conversation, refreshment and relaxation in leisure hours. If the times were more leisurely than those when established clubs grew popular, the time spent in coffee-houses was correspondingly greater, whole days being passed in them, while in some faro and other gambling games flourished in the late and small hours. The beverages of coffee and chocolate which gave their names to the houses in many cases were the only ones served; in other houses wine and liquor of all kinds were obtainable. As many as three thousand such houses flourished in London during the century, almost every one boasting some individual distinction and a clientele particularly its own. One or two would be held sacred to men of letters, others to painters, the army, the navy or to merchants in certain branches of trade. Often the *habitué*s of a coffee-house were known as its members, though in fact there was no established system of membership, the term implying no more than a regular patronage. Grouped about Pall Mall and St. James's Street were many of the houses of highest reputation, some of which—like White's Chocolate House—were to bequeath their names to West End clubs succeeding them in later years, while others further afield in the City or Soho catered for men of varied callings and classes. It was to the coffee-houses rather than to any other institutions that enquiring visitors to London made their first visits, knowing that there could be found the best entertainment the town had to offer; and to quote from John Macky's *A Journey Through England*, published in 1714, the year which saw the first George succeed Anne on the throne, is to note but one of many such pictures of London life:

I am lodged in the street called Pall Mall, the ordinary residence of all strangers because of its vicinity to the Queen's Palace, the Park, the Parliament House, the Theatres and the Chocolate and Coffee-houses, where the best company frequent. . . . About twelve the *beau monde* assemble in several coffee or chocolate-houses; the best of which are the Cocoa-tree and White's Chocolate-houses, St. James's, the Smyrna, Mrs. Rochford's and the British Coffee-houses, and all these are so near one another that in less than an hour you see the company of them all. We are carried to these places in chairs [sedans] which are here very cheap, a guinea a week or a shilling an hour, and your chairmen serve you for porters to run on errands, as your gondoliers do in Venice. . . . You are entertained at picquet or basset at White's, or you may talk politics at the Smyrna or St. James's . . . the parties have their different places, where, however, a stranger is always well received; but a Whig will no more go to the Cocoa-tree than a Tory will be seen at the Coffee-house St. James's.

The Scots generally go to the British, and a mixture of all sorts to the Smyrna. There are other little coffee-houses much frequented in this neighbourhood. Young Man's for officers. Old Man's for stock jobbers, paymasters and courtiers; and Little Man's for sharpers. . . .

To the names of houses given in this extract might be added many more that were to become known as favoured haunts of the eminent. Button's and Will's coffee-houses had among their regular frequenters a long list of literary figures that included Dryden, Addison, Swift, Steele and Pope. Dryden died before the best days of the coffee-house, but in his last years spent much of his time at Will's, sitting always in a chair kept especially for him in the window in summer-time, and by the fire in winter, young men of literary aspirations going to the house in the hope of receiving the honour of a few words from him or of being offered a pinch from his snuff-box. Of Addison it was said that the greater part of his bachelor life was spent at Button's. It was at the Piazza Coffee-House that Sheridan might be found; and at the Bedford, Henry Fielding. Goldsmith more often used the St. James's, which shared with the Smyrna, British and Bedford the patronage of most of the wits of the age. Publishers and those who dealt in books and bookish matters held their own court at the Chapter House. To Old Slaughter's came many writers and even more painters; among the latter Hogarth, Hayman, Oman, Gainsborough and Richard Wilson.

If associations with eminent names have left many coffee-houses with high reputations history does not

c

overlook those that were shady by comparison—that Little Man's, for instance, which was noted 'for sharpers', was no better than a gambling den notorious for crooked play at faro. Of Old Man's, which was in Scotland Yard, Ned Ward, author of the *Secret History of Clubs*, has left an illuminating description, both of the place and of the type of 'courtiers' who frequented it, and has not forgotten the importance attached by these little gentlemen to snuff:

> We now ascended a pair of stairs, which brought us into an old-fashioned room, where a gaudy crowd of odoriferous Tom-Essences were walking backwards and forwards, with their hats in their hands, not daring to convert them to their intended use, lest it should put the fore-tops of their wigs into some disorder. . . . We sat down, observed it was a great rarity to hear anybody call for a dish of Politician's Porridge, or any other liquor, as it was to hear a beau call for a pipe of tobacco; their whole exercise being to charge and discharge their nostrils and keep the curls of their periwigs in their proper order. The clashing of their snush-box lids, in opening and shutting, made more noise than their tongues. . . .

In such company, it is further recorded, the calling for tobacco and lighting of pipes by the intruders caused so much disgust that 'several Sir Foplins drew their faces into as many peevish wrinkles as the beaux of the Bow Street Coffee-house, near Covent Garden, did when the gentleman in masquerade came in among them'.

Ward's picture of Old Man's and its *habitués* no doubt would have fitted equally well many other coffee-houses of the kind supported by such coxcombs as found relaxation in the 'Court of Honour' of which the secretary was Monsieur Lillie, perfumer and authority on the blending of snuff. The eighteenth century exquisite so much associated with the history of the coffee-houses makes many appearances in literature with his snuff-box

accompanying him as the symbol of his race and age. In
The Downfall of Dancing he laments:

> My gold lac'd Vest, of green Velour,
> So wondrous gay and nice;
> My Silver Snuff-box figur'd o'er,
> And Lid of Smart Device,
> My Chevron'd Clocks and Silk-bound Shoes
> Are thrown aside, no more for use.

And Thomas Baker holds him up to ridicule in the play,
Tunbridge Walks (1703):

> But the surprizing Joy when two Fops meet in the Side-box,
> tho' they parted but two minutes before at a Chocolate House;
> the Side-Bow, the Embrace; and the fulsome Trick you men
> have got of kissing one another . . . the Toss o' the Head, the
> Airs o' the Snuff-box, and the leer at an Actress on the Stage.

It was, perhaps, with this sort of frequenter in mind
that the *Tatler* solemnly advised its readers to enter a
coffee-house only after 'preparing the body with three
dishes of Bohea [tea] and purging the brains with two
pinches of snuff'.

Refreshingly solid by comparison was the company to
be met with at the Turk's Head, a Soho coffee-house.
Here weight and wisdom were well represented among
the patrons in general, and in particular by Dr Samuel
Johnson, whose addiction to coffee-houses was hardly
less than his devotion to taverns and inns. Catholic in
his patronage, he shared with his friend Garrick a liking
for Old Slaughter's and used also the St. James's, the
Bedford, and Peele's in Fleet Street; but probably he
was seen most often at the Turk's Head, taking, as a
stimulus to conversation, snuff which he fished out of
his waistcoat pocket in enormous pinches.

Unlike nearly all his coterie and contemporaries, he
had abandoned the carrying of a snuff-box in favour of
having a pocket filled with a supply of loose snuff

adequate to his needs. In this he was like Frederick the
Great of Prussia, whose tremendous consumption of
snuff was proverbial and who not only had a leather-
lined pocket made in each of his waistcoats that he might
carry his snuff loose and help himself without loss of
time but insisted, also, that a box of fresh snuff was kept
in every room of whatever palace he was occupying.
'That box is not big enough for us both—keep it!'
Frederick said on one occasion to a servant whom he
caught abstracting a surreptitious pinch from one of the
palace boxes. In spite of the amount he took it is possible
that Frederick the Great was able to keep himself—or
was kept—reasonably free of snuff on his clothes and
face, a distinction Dr Johnson could not claim to share.
Notoriously untidy and careless of his personal appearance, he was often to be seen bearing abundant traces of
snuff on lip and waistcoat.

Passing references to Johnson's use of snuff are
numerous enough to have left his name associated perhaps more than any other with devotion to the habit,
though nearly every leading figure of his time was as
heavy a snuff-taker. Often to be portrayed in later years
with a snuff-box in his hand or open on the table before
him, Johnson ranks almost as a symbol of the eighteenth
century age of snuffing, even having a snuff-shop named
after him. He is remembered as often as a snuffy figure as
he is as a lexicographer, a patron of taverns and coffee-
houses, a member of the Beefsteak Club or a visitor to
the theatre. A friend of Leigh Hunt's it was who 'knew
a lady who remembered Dr Johnson in the pit taking
snuff out of his waistcoat pocket' in the intervals of
going into the green-room to see his friend and former
pupil, David Garrick.

Not until 1773 did Johnson himself write, 'Smoking
has gone out. To be sure, it is a shocking thing, blowing
smoke out of our mouths into other people's mouths,

eyes and noses, and having the same thing done to us'. Long before then snuff had enslaved England to an extent which can be compared with the cigarette-smoking craze of a century and a half later. Gradually snuff-taking had succeeded smoking with every class, the lower orders copying society in this as in most other fashions, however great might be the ridicule attached to the affected mannerisms of snuffing practised by both sexes in London's leisured class. The latter had even produced schools of etiquette which gave instruction in the finer points of taking snuff, apparently studying the handling of a snuff-box with the same seriousness that was allowed to the manipulation of a fan, and supporting such professors as one who advertised in the *Spectator* in 1711:

> The exercise of the Snuff-box, according to the most fashionable Airs and Notions, in opposition to the exercise of the Fan, will be taught, with the best plain or perfumed Snuff . . .

Pope marked this same association of fan and snuff-box when he wrote:

> Snuff or the fan supply each pause of chat,
> With singing, laughing, ogling and all that.

Britain's passion for snuff was shared at this period by nearly every country in Europe, and it is in 1720 that we find one of the most entertaining summings-up of the situation given by a German, Johann Cohausen, in a satirical piece of writing called *The Lust of the Longing Nose*:

> The world has taken up a ridiculous fashion—the excessive use of snuff. All nations are snuffing. All classes snuff, from the highest to the lowest. I have sometimes wondered to see how lords and lackeys, High Society and the mob, woodchoppers and handy men, broom-squires and beadles, take out their snuff-boxes with an air, and dip into them. Both sexes snuff, for the fashion has spread to women; the ladies began it, and are now imitated by the washerwomen. People snuff so often that their noses are more like a dust-heap than a nose; so irrationally that they think the

dust an ornament, although, since the world began, all rational men have thought a dirty face unhealthy; so recklessly that they lose the sense of smell and their bodily health.

They snuff without need, at all times, in all places, without rest, as though their fate and fortune, their name and fame, their life and health, even their eternal salvation depended upon it.

Do but notice what grimaces snuff-takers make, how their features are convulsed, how they dip into their snuff boxes in measured rhythm, cock up their noses, compose their mouths, eyes and all their features to a pompous dignity, and, as they perform the solemn rite of snuff-taking, they look as if they scorned the whole world, or were bent on some enterprise of which they might say, like Bouflet, 'I will make the whole world tremble!'

I have found, by certain experiments, that such men have the idea that, in the moment when they sniff the snuff up their noses, they are as men inspired, transformed into mighty kings and princes, or at least made royal and princely at heart.

Nor was Cohausen the only critic to make clear his dislike of snuff and snuff-takers. From time to time, as snuffing spread ever further, voices of protest were heard, some of them still trying to assert that the habit was a harmful one. F. W. Fairholt, in his *Tobacco, Its History and Associations* (1859), recalls that 'grave doctors were not wanting to declare that the brains of snuff-takers were found after death dried to a sort of dirty membrane, clogged with soot'. Perhaps some of these medical authorities were better qualified to give an opinion than John Hill, who was loud in his denunciation of snuff in England, at the height of its popularity in 1761. Hill described himself as a doctor and liked best to be known as 'Sir' John Hill; in fact he was a quack apothecary who lived and practised in James Street, Covent Garden, and whose claim to a title was that of having been made a knight of the Swedish order of Vasa. This distinction was given him as the author of a book called *The Vegetable System* various other works of his dealt with botany and horticulture and he edited the *British Magazine* (1746–50), in the pages of which and other journals he was accustomed to pillory anyone or anything incurring his displeasure. At various times he attacked Henry Fielding, the Royal Society, snuff and David Garrick. Of snuff he said that 'many persons have perished miserably of diseases occasioned, or rendered incurable, by its use'. David Garrick, a hardened snuff-taker, pronounced his opinion of Hill in an epigram:

> For physics and farces, his equal there scarce is.
> His farces are physic, his physic a farce is.

All such indictments against snuff, however, were laughed at by the thousands who preferred the inconsiderable risk of dying of snuff to the misery of attempting to live without it. If a few doctors condemned snuff, the faculty in general were confirmed snuffers. So were clerics and divines of all persuasions. Habitually the clergy took snuff while conducting services, and preached with snuff-box in hand. Of one incumbent of a rural parish it was related that he became so distraught from want of snuff at a time when a supply was unobtainable in his remote village, that his sanity was saved only by the presence of mind of his clerk. The latter, bethinking him of the quantity of snuff normally spilt and scattered about the pulpit in the course of a Sunday sermon, filled a box with sweepings from the church floor; this mixture he took to his vicar, who pronounced it an excellent snuff substitute in which the proportion of dust was but slight and quite tolerable. The story has its parallel in the legend of a country parson of an earlier day, whose dependence on smoking was almost as great and who found himself similarly deprived of tobacco. He, it is said, temporarily but satisfactorily alleviated his longing for a pipe by smoking hemp cut from his church bell-ropes.

Even papal sanction was given to snuff-taking in Roman Catholic churches in mid-eighteenth century. According to Count Corti's *History of Smoking* (1931), Pope Benedict XIII, who himself was a snuff-taker and had been a smoker, had noticed the frequency with which some of his clergy left church during services to refresh themselves from their snuff-boxes; to prevent these interruptions he annulled the snuffing ban imposed a century earlier.

The wholehearted enthusiasm with which women had taken to the snuff habit incurred its share of comment, much of it from men moved to protest not so much against women taking snuff as against their taking it to excess and on unsuitable occasions. Addison, living as he did in a word of snuff-takers, was yet disgusted at the frequency with which a lady of fashion 'pulls out her box of good Brazile' while in church. Writing in the *Spectator*, he deplored that 'to show the audacity of a well-bred woman she offers her snuff-box to men as well as women sitting near her'. Such complaints and appeals for moderation had the usual effect—none; unless it was to increase the feminine fondness for a habit that appealed, for obvious reasons, far more strongly than pipe-smoking had done to women of the previous century. Tobacco taken as snuff might lack the soothing, steadying quality of smoked tobacco; it had instead an invigorating, freshening effect, sharply if very temporarily stimulating to the brain and thoughts. Begun by Englishwomen as a mere fashion among those in high places, by ladies of the Court and in London society, snuffing was a habit more easily acquired than dropped; in a pinch of snuff was a lightning tonic for flagging spirits, a stimulus in conversation, at cards or social gatherings; in the acceptance or offering of a pinch was a polished gesture and a practised accomplishment; and in the endless varieties of perfumed snuffs could be

I Wooden Figure of a Highlander taking
snuff, traditional Sign of the Snuff-seller

II A London Snuff-shop

incorporated almost every form of scent beloved of womankind. Copied from ladies of high society by those a step lower in the social scale, snuff-taking reached all classes until, as Besant put it, 'women who hawked things with a wheel-barrow, fishwives, nurses and others, all carried snuff-boxes'. In the cheap, portable and ever ready luxury of snuff, albeit snuff considerably stronger and much less aromatic and refined than that taken by ladies of fashion, working women of the eighteenth century found a comfort and a pick-me-up, the place of which was to be filled to a large extent by the ubiquitous cup of tea in later years when the cheapness of tea brought it within the means of nearly everyone.

The degree to which certain great ladies became the slaves of their snuff-boxes is well known: notably Queen Charlotte, George III's consort, and Lady Mary Wortley Montagu, remembered as much for her famous quarrel with Alexander Pope as on account of her writings, are among those who make extremely snuffy appearances in history. For evidence that—though their historical significance has made it particularly memorable—their indulgence was no greater than that of countless other eighteenth century Englishwomen of all classes, we can accept if we like the statements made in 1782 by 'A Friend to Female Beauty', the writer of a pamphlet called *Free Thoughts on Snuff-Taking*:

> Who, without regret, can see an agreeable and well-dressed Lady with a beautiful Countenance, elegant Symmetry, and fine natural colouring of the Features, pull off a glove, and, with a fine, white, delicate hand, take out a box, and put her pretty thumb and finger into a nasty-coloured powder, and apply the same to a beautiful Face and spoil it, by changing the fine natural colour of the Skin in more places than where this filthy drug is laid on, and causing the blood to rise into the face by coughing, etc.? This is not uncommon even to those constantly addicted to this nauseous custom!
>
> But they all do it! Little Miss would never have thought of

snuff-taking if she had not seen her Mother and old maiden Aunt do it before her, and Betty the Chamber-maid, Molly the House-maid, and Mrs. Cook would never have thought of buying Snuff-boxes but to imitate their Mistress; and the girl next door, just from the country, seeing Miss Molly, while washing the stone steps at the door, set down her mop to take a pinch of Snuff, thinks all London maids do likewise, and she to be sure must resemble them. She conquers the first difficulty of it and con-tinues it, even in old age, when with poverty, sluttishness, and dram-drinking added to it, make her as disagreeable an object as any Female possibly can be.

There were, however, among women snuff-takers many who managed to indulge the habit tidily, without meriting such strictures as those of the 'Friend to Female Beauty'; some even were fastidious enough to take their snuff from little spoons, thus keeping their finger-nails unsoiled by following the plan of the Chinese, who dipped their snuff in spoonfuls from little bottles rather than boxes. This way of taking snuff is remembered in the lines:

> To such a height with some is fashion grown
> They feed their very nostrils with a spoon.

Of more usual methods of snuffing there were several. The commonest was to insert the forefinger and thumb of the right hand into the box, held in the left hand, and raise a pinch directly to each nostril, the box having been prepared for opening by a tap or two upon the top to free any snuff adhering to the hinge or underneath the lid. Occasionally followed by ladies was the practice of placing a little snuff on the back of a finger-nail, from which it was delicately sniffed. Less often employed by the initiated snuffer than by the beginner was the taking from the back of the left hand of a pinch placed there with the right forefinger and thumb. The act of snuffing or inhaling was performed in polite society without noise, grimace, or ugly upward thrust of finger or thumb when they were applied to the nose. For spilling snuff on clothes or lip there was little excuse except in carelessness: the handkerchief—first introduced by snuff-takers—was employed lightly to flick away any traces of snuff, as well as for its normal purpose, immediately after the pinch was taken. It was in the neglect of this care—in the untidiness of spilt snuff, the ugliness of unnecessary facial contortion and the vulgarity of an audible sniff—that snuff-taking eventually came to acquire the name of 'a dirty habit'. Particularly has this overworked description clung to snuffing since the world discovered the cleanliness of universally disseminated cigarette smoke, with the ash, stains and occasional burns that accompany it.

Some five years before the printing of *Free Thoughts on Snuff-Taking* (1782) there occurred in London the death of a certain Mrs Thompson, a lady whose devotion to snuff might have served the pamphlet's author as a fearful example. Details of Mrs Thompson's life have gone unrecorded, perhaps because in the age of snuffing in which she lived there was nothing unusual in her indulgence, but in her Will she expressed sentiments and wishes which surely deserve a place of honour in snuff history:

IN THE NAME OF GOD. AMEN

I, Margaret Thompson . . . being of sound mind, do desire that when my soul is departed from this wicked world, my body and effects may be disposed of in the manner following. . . .

I also desire that all my handkerchiefs that I may have unwashed at the time of my decease, after they have been got together by my old and trusty servant, Sarah Stewart, be put by her, and her alone, at the bottom of my coffin, which I desire may be made large enough for that purpose, together with such a quantity of the best Scotch snuff (in which she knoweth I always had the greatest delight) as will cover my deceased body; and this I desire, and more especially as it is usual to put flowers into the coffins of departed friends, and nothing can be so pleasant and refreshing to me as that precious powder. But I strictly charge that no one be suffered to approach my body till the coffin is closed, and it is necessary to carry me to my burial, which I order in the following manner:—

Six men to be my bearers, who are well known to be great snuff-takers in the parish of St. James's, Westminster; and instead of mourning, each to wear a snuff-coloured beaver, which I desire to be bought for that purpose, and given to them. Six Maidens of my old acquaintance to bear my pall, each to wear a proper hood, and to carry a box filled with the best Scotch snuff, to take for their refreshment as they go along. Before my corpse I desire that the minister may be invited to walk, and to take a certain quantity of snuff, not exceeding one pound, to whom I also bequeath five guineas on condition of his doing so.

And I also desire my old and faithful servant, Sarah Stewart, to walk before the corpse to distribute every twenty yards a large handful of Scotch snuff on the ground, and to the crowd who possibly may follow me to my burial place, on condition I bequeath her £20. And I also desire that at least two bushels of the said snuff shall be distributed at the door of my house in Boyle Street.

I desire, also, that my funeral shall be at twelve o'clock at noon. And in addition to the various legacies I have left my friends in a former will, I desire that to each person there shall be given a pound of the best Scotch snuff, as it is the grand cordial of human nature.

Mrs Thompson's home was in Boyle Street, Burlington Gardens, though a Scottish origin is suggested by her name and that of her faithful servant as well as by her insistence on Scotch snuff. References to the nature of Scotch snuff and to the mulls used as snuff-boxes in Scotland are best left to their appropriate chapters, but it should be noted here that the average Scot's fondness for snuff had become almost proverbial in England at the time when Mrs Thompson's Will was made. Though Scotland was a snuff-taking country long before the habit was generally adopted south of the Border, it was not until the rebellions of 1715 and 1745 that English attention was drawn to the Scottish way of life, particularly to an allegedly unbounded indulgence in *sneish*, *snishon*, *snichen* and a variety of other Gaelic renderings of the word snuff. 'Thy vile snichen' is an expression occurring in the poems of R. Smith in 1714; Ramsay wrote ten years later of 'a mill of good snishing to prie', and endless other contemporary allusions support the eighteenth century Scotsman's character as a snuffer, though there is a certain humour about his having been chosen as a symbol of the snuff trade in an England grown altogether as steeped in snuff as Scotland.

A wooden effigy of a Highlander in the act of dipping into his horn snuff-mull or raising a pinch to his nose was by far the commonest of the signs indicating a shop where snuff was sold; in various forms Highlanders appeared outside the premises of snuffmen all over England in the eighteenth century, and in a few cases still remain in use. The earlier examples of these signs were carved and coloured with a care giving them a distinction hardly shared by many that were to appear later, all very much alike and of crude workmanship. One of the first, perhaps the first of all, to be set up in London portrayed a slim young Highlander, probably intended to represent the Pretender and having a particular significance in marking a house said to have been a Jacobite meeting place. This was David Wishart's snuff shop in Coventry Street, in existence in 1720, where business was carried on under a sign of which the Highland figure formed only a part, the other components being a thistle and a crown equally suggestive of Jacobite sympathies. Not until 1880 were Wishart's old premises pulled down, when the business—by then concerned more with tobacco than snuff—was transferred to its present shop in Panton Street. Following Wishart's example other snuffmen adopted as their signs figures of Highlanders in great variety of highly-coloured kilts and plaids until the streets of London and most English cities were dotted with them, either of bellicose aspect—as many were at first—with claymores in their hands, or settled in their later stereotyped gesture of snuff-taking. One of several noted by Sir Ambrose Heal in his *The Signboards of Old London Shops* was William Hebb, who sold snuff about the year 1763 at "Ye Highlander, ye corner of Pall Mall, facing St. James's, Hay Market', but who in 1772 was to be found 'at the Old Highlander next door to Mr Pinchbeck's, at the corner of Cockspur Street, facing the Hay Market'. The same address might well be indicated by both descriptions, though it is clear that Mr Hebb's Highlander had aged rapidly in seven years; perhaps because of the appearance of a younger rival at some neighbouring shop.

Less common than Highlanders but sometimes used by snuff-sellers were such signs as Indians (intended to be Brazilian), Twin Nigger Boys, Negro's Heads, Daggers, the Green Man and Still, and various designs incorporating the Rasp or Grater of old snuff association. The numbers of snuffmen in business in London alone during the eighteenth century suggest the extent of snuff-taking and support the assertion made by one critic of the habit that more hands were employed in this trade than in any other in the country. Though many concerned in the business were merely salesmen of snuff, others were importers of foreign varieties which in some cases they blended or flavoured before retailing, and some were actual grinders of rappees and other English snuffs. Claims to have been manufacturers as well as sellers of snuff occur often on trade tokens issued in the later part of the century when token coinage was flourishing, and such coins recall the existence of a whole tribe of modest snuff traders whose businesses were neither long lived nor important enough to earn a record elsewhere; such little business as, for instance, that of John Hayward, of Tooley Street, who manufactured

'Fancy Snuffs', or that of James Bean, who dealt in 'Genuine Tobacco & Snuff, Wholesale & Retail' at Black Prince Row. Two of the lesser dealers in the same commodities achieved a modest fame in their day from the slogans they displayed as shop signs. One of the two for many years had carried on a thriving snuff and tobacco trade on Fish Street Hill with little or no local opposition, when the other opened a rival shop across the road. The newcomer, whose name was Farr, at first did little business, but eventually ensnared a considerable proportion of his opponent's customers by erecting a magnificent sign bearing in gold letters the words 'The Best Snuff and Tobacco by Farr'. To this the old established snuffman replied in due course with an even more spectacular erection, boldly claiming to supply 'Far Better Snuff and Tobacco than the Best by Farr'; thereby, it is said, recovering the patronage he had lost.

Of the firms pursuing the manufacturing and wholesale snuff trade within the City of London none was better known than James Taddy & Company, established in or about the year 1740. Taddy's snuffs attained a high reputation in the second half of the eighteenth century and were destined to keep it for over a century thereafter, until in fact as late as 1920, when a strike caused the firm to abandon a business that had flourished for the greater part of two hundred years, at first in Fenchurch Street and then for more than a century in the Minories. At one time the name Taddy was almost a synonym for snuff in London in much the way that Lundy Foot[1] was in Dublin, the products of both firms being equally noticed in the literature of their heyday.

Perhaps the most remarkable man among snuff-traders east of Temple Bar during the eighteenth century was John Hardham, well known as a blender and retailer at the sign of the Red Lyon in Fleet Street at the time when

---

[1] *Vide* chapter iv.

Taddy's business began. Beginning his career as a servant, Hardham eventually made a name for himself in London, as much as a philanthropist and a personality in the world of the theatre as for his various popular snuffs, by far the most famous of which was his '37'. Writing of Fleet Street in *The Town*, Leigh Hunt quoted Baker's *Biographia Dramatica* of 1782 on the subjects of Hardham's life and business:

> On the same side of the way as Shoe Lane, but nearer Fleet Market, was Hardham's, a celebrated snuff-shop, the founder of which deserves mention for a very delicate generosity. He was numberer at Drury Lane Theatre, that is to say, the person who counted the number of people in the house, from a hole over the top of the stage; a practice now discontinued. Whether this employment led him to number snuffs, as well as men, we cannot say, but he was the first who gave them their distinctions that way. Lovers of 'The pungent grains of titillating dust' are indebted to him for the famous compound entitled '37'.
>
> 'Being passionately fond of theatrical entertainments, he was seldom,' says his biographer, 'without embryo Richards and Hotspurs strutting and bellowing in his dining-room, or in the parlour behind his shop. The latter of these apartments was adorned with heads of most of the persons celebrated for dramatic excellence; and to these he frequently referred in the course of his instructions.'
>
> 'There is one circumstance, however, in his private character,' continues our authority, 'which deserves honourable rescue. . . . His charity was extensive in an uncommon degree and was conveyed to many of its objects in a most delicate manner. On account of his known integrity (for he once failed in business more creditably than he could have made a fortune by it) he was often entrusted with the care of paying little annual stipends to unfortunate women, and others who were in equal want of relief; and he has been known of his generosity . . . to continue these advances long after the sources of them stopped by death . . . indeed his purse was never shut, even to those who were casually recommended by his common acquaintance.'

To his other accomplishments the versatile John Hardham added those of acting occasionally in minor parts and of writing at least one comedy. David Garrick was one of his customers at the Fleet Street shop and is thought to have done much toward popularising the No. 37 snuff by mentioning it on the stage when one of his parts included the offering of a pinch of snuff to another actor. In time Hardham's 37 became so widely known and liked that its sale spread far beyond the bounds of Fleet Street, its blender supplying it in bulk to other snuffmen in the retail trade, while taking care that none of them discovered the secret of its flavouring. From time to time various ingenious suggestions were advanced to explain the reason for naming so successful a snuff with a mere number, among them a theory that no fewer than thirty-seven different ingredients went to its making; another, that its title was given it by the Marquis of Townshend, a customer of Hardham's, when a majority of thirty-seven votes had enabled him to triumph in an election. In fact the reason was the simple one implied by Leigh Hunt, that Hardham's habit was to number each of the many blends he originated, storing them in jars ranged in numerical order on the shelves of his shop; in this way avoiding any confusion which might have arisen among shopmen and customers if his wares had been labelled with the elaborate names borne by many snuffs of the period. Numbers 5 and 18 were other blends which an old invoice shows Hardham to have been selling in 1762, and doubtless he concocted for various clients and indicated by numbers some dozens of such mixtures. A variety of flavours could be produced by blending in differing proportions several standard sorts of snuff, and endless possibilities were open to blenders like Hardham who added perfumes and flower essences.

Number 37 and his other less well-known snuffs made a fortune for John Hardham, and in spite of his continued generosity he died (in 1772) a rich man. In his Will, in which he described himself as a Tobacconist and Snuff

D

Merchant of the Parish of St. Bride in Fleet Street, he left the interest on £20,000 to a lady referred to by Hunt as 'a female acquaintance', on whose death the principal passed to the relief of the poor of Chichester, the testator's native city. His business, sold for the first time immediately after his death, was destined to change hands several times, and its situation once, in the course of its history. Now on the south side of Fleet Street, hard by Ludgate Circus, the shop still does a revealingly large trade in snuff as well as smoking tobacco; outwardly it is distinguished by the honoured name of John Hardham and his old address 'at the sign of the Red Lyon', and inwardly by its shelves of brown earthenware snuff-jars, a cabinet formerly containing essences and perfumes used in snuff flavouring, and by other relics of its founder.

Elsewhere in Fleet Street, on the northern side, another snuff business of eighteenth century origin, Radford's, contains a further link with Hardham in the sign used by his apprentice, William Hoare. The latter, it appears, set up as a snuffman on his own account after his master's death, using as a sign this old metal plate painted with the words:

Wm. Hoare
Snuff Maker
was the Only
Apprentice
to Mr. Jno.
Hardham
Deceased.

The fingers of one hand would more than suffice to count the London businesses of eighteenth century origin which are still actively engaged in the blending and selling of snuff. The West End contains one for which this claim could be made, the snuff house of Fribourg & Treyer in the Haymarket. Originally distinguished by its sign, the Rasp and Crown of old snuff associations, the Fribourg & Treyer shop has become a landmark in modern London by reason ·of its unique appearance. Outwardly its twin bow-windows of many small panes, set between the original curving brass plates below and the gold-painted legends of ancient 'Royal Appointments' above, and divided by their little flight of steps leading up from the Haymarket pavement, appear today very much as they did in the heyday of snuff-taking. Within, the front shop and back room are still divided by the graceful Adam screen known to countless customers for snuff in the past, and behind the old oak counter can be seen shelves worn thin in places by two centuries of constant removal and replacement of earthen snuff-jars. Otherwise remarkable for several reasons, the Haymarket snuff house is particularly distinguished in having prepared and sold snuff uninterruptedly for more than two-and-a-quarter centuries, for the greater part of which period the business has remained the concern and pride of several generations of one family. Throughout the more interesting and historically important of these years of trading, ledgers and other manuscript records were kept. Almost certainly the most revealing snuff documents extant, these books disclose more of the history of fashionable snuff-taking than do any published works.

Our first references to distinguished snuffers and snuffs figuring in Fribourg & Treyer's records should be introduced by an outline of the firm's origin and ownership, a story told at length and in detail by George Evans in his *The Old Snuff House of Fribourg & Treyer*, published privately in 1921 to commemorate two centuries of trade in the Haymarket. It was in 1720 that the business was founded under the sign of the Rasp and Crown by one Peter Fribourg. Thereafter it was known as 'Fribourg's' for some sixty years; until in fact the year 1780, when, with G. A. Treyer as its sole proprietor, it emerged under the style of Fribourg & Treyer. Still using the old Rasp and Crown sign, Treyer carried on at the present shop, No. 34 Haymarket, an extensive trade in snuff for twenty-three years, being ably assisted the while by his wife, Martha. Through this Mrs Martha Treyer—by birth a Miss Evans—the snuff house passed to the Evans family in 1803, since when it has had no other owners or administrators than successive generations of the same family.

Early in its history the Haymarket snuff house acquired a reputation for supplying and blending the finer varieties of snuff (mainly, though not entirely, the imported kinds) and began to count among its customers a number of the connoisseurs of that time. Within the eighteenth century appeared the first of many literary references to the house as the source of snuffs used by memorable men and women. One such note, made by John Pinkerton in his *Walpoliana* of 1799, discloses Horace Walpole's choice of snuff and his method of keeping it at Strawberry Hill, Twickenham, which became his home in 1747 and thereafter came to be considered the virtual centre of fashionable learning in England:

> After his coffee he tasted nothing; but his snuff-box of *tabac d'étrennes*, from Fribourg's, was not forgotten, and was replenished from a cannister lodged in an ancient marble urn of great thickness, which stood in the window-seat, and served to secure its moisture and rich flavour.

The surviving ledgers and trade records of the Haymarket snuff house begin with certain day-book entries made in the year 1764. From the first these jotted notes in faded ink record the varieties of snuff most fashionable at that period, together with the names of the clients who bought them, the quantities they used and the prices they paid. Of most frequent occurrence are sales of foreign snuffs (imported by the firm and sold either unmixed or blended), usually bearing the names of the countries or cities of their origin; constantly appearing are the names

of French, German, Dutch, Spanish and Brazilian snuffs
which held their popularity throughout the age of
fashionable snuffing. Rappees, which in some cases were
ground in England from imported tobaccos, take second
place to the snuffs ground and prepared abroad; and only
occasionally do Irish or Scotch kinds figure among the
choices of English society. Coarse, medium or fine grind-
ings are indicated by prefixes or affixes in either English
or French, and sometimes by abbreviations; as when, on
26 September 1764, Lord George Beauclerck was noted
as the purchaser of '1 lb. Paris F.' at 6s., this being a *Fin*
or fine-ground snuff as opposed to one of *Gros* or *Demi-
gros* grain. From its price this particular snuff appears to
have been one of exceptional quality or merit, as more
often recorded at the same time are varieties priced at four
and five shillings the pound; approximately, one may note
in passing, the same cost as that of an ounce of snuff in
the present day. To this client's account is added, as in
most other cases, the cost of the canister in which the
snuff was packed—6d. for a one-pound canister, or a
shilling for a 'double canister' holding two pounds—and
a charge of 2d. for 'booking'.

After nearly two centuries it is as illuminating to note
the quantities bought as the prices paid. 'September 14th,
1764, Captain Sam Hood, 6 lbs. Rappee at 5s.' (in three
double canisters, three shillings) is by no means an
unusually large order, heavy snuff-takers normally buying
more than this at a time. References to despatch to
country places by coach are frequent throughout the
books, and other methods of delivery or the messengers
to whom snuff was handed on the customer's order are
carefully noted. John Williams, Esq., of Hall Grove, who
had a pound of Coarse *Carotte* on 18 April 1764, and a
pound of Dutch snuff in a leaden canister in September
of the same year, wished it 'delivered to Miss Hews';
while Mr. Frederick Harbest's modest half-crown's worth

of Dunkirk and Rappee was sent to him care of the Duke of Cumberland. Sedan-chairmen often were employed by London customers sending hurriedly for snuff supplies and are remembered in many such entries as 'delivered to chairman'; but only one is distinguished by the cryptic comment 'chairwoman with whiskers'!

Women make regular appearances as customers for snuff in the Haymarket ledgers, their orders being in fair proportion to those of men and showing as wide a variety of tastes. At the very beginning of the first volume may be read, '1764, July 19th., Dutchess [sic] of Grafton, ½ lb. French. 2s. 6d.'; and early in the following year, 'Lady Suffolk. 1 lb. Misipi [Mississippi] 4s. 0d.' Until the year 1778 a constant succession of such entries record the firm's patronage by snuff-takers, both men and women, in the higher walks of life. A gap occurring in the day books between 1778 and 1795 leaves the snuff-house's retail trade for that period unchronicled, but other surviving manuscripts and casual notes serve to suggest a continued expansion of business and to illustrate the varied ramifications of successful snuff trading in London. A note in 1789 throws a light on the scale of the firm's imports of foreign snuffs, Custom House payments of £245 2s. 8d. for 'Excise', and £153 4s. 2d. for 'Custom' being made on sundry casks, together with expenses amounting to £6 7s. 4d. Beyond the importation, blending and retailing aspects of the business were those of producing English snuff by milling imported tobacco and reducing to powder such snuff as reached this country in the form of *carottes*. One memorandum dated 23 April 1791 shows that six hundred and ninety-one pounds of British Rappee 'came from the Mill' on that day, the tobacco which produced this quantity of snuff having weighed seven hundred and thirty-eight pounds 'when it went to the Mill'. Another mentions that the grinding of twenty *carottes* produced sixty-four pounds of snuff. A third, headed 'Snuff work Declared', deals with home-produced snuffs 'For to be Laid Down'; the quantities being 'For British Rappee, 2000 lb, For Scotch, 200 lb, For Short Cut, 54 lb'. Yet other branches of the many-sided business embraced the export of considerable quantities of snuff to clients and agents abroad, and the retailing of several famous kinds of snuff prepared by other firms. Among the latter were the popular 37 from Hardham's and some of the Irish high-dried specialities of the Dublin snuffman, Lundy Foot.

Figuring in the list of the firm's customers at this time were several of the more celebrated snuff-taking patrons of coffee-houses mentioned earlier in this chapter; notably Garrick, who was by no means alone in dividing his patronage between Hardham in the City and Treyer in the West End. The close association of coffee-houses with snuff-taking was maintained as long as the former kept their place in social life, and even when fashionable frequenters of coffee-houses became fewer in the later years of the century the surviving houses found a fresh type of patron who long before had adopted snuff as an essential comfort. Rather than in the circles of literature, art, politics or leisure, these latter day coffee-houses found their support among lesser merchants, shopkeepers, ambitious apprentices and artisans who were less concerned with forgathering to gossip and pass the time away agreeably than with reading the news. Like other habits, snuff-taking and coffee-housing included, newspaper reading had spread from the upper classes to the lower; but newspapers were expensive luxuries to buy, with *The Times* costing the considerable sum of sixpence daily, the *True Briton* as much, and the four scanty pages of *Johnson's British Weekly* fourpence-halfpenny. The cheapest way to read the news of the day was to drop in at a coffee-house where newspapers were supplied for the use of customers, with no more to pay than the cost of a cup of coffee.

While many of the houses thus continued to exist with customers taking their coffee and snuff in an atmosphere of steady and altogether dull respectability, others went out of business for lack of support as the century drew to a close. Others again survived in another form, emerging as clubs; the word club gradually acquiring its modern implication of a permanent house of call with a large elected membership, and losing in part its earlier meaning of a body or society meeting occasionally at a tavern or hired room for the purposes of dining, wining or discussion.

West End clubs were to prove good customers to snuffmen in the St. James's district. Among the early members of such clubs as White's, Brooks's and Boodle's were many men to whom fine snuffs were as important a part of life as fine wines, and to this day may be seen in a few old clubs survivors of the communal snuff-boxes which once stood on morning- and dining-room chimney-pieces and side-tables, convenient for the members' use. Of large capacity, some of these club boxes were divided into compartments each containing a different blend, while others held but one—an especially blended 'Club Snuff'; one such blend became well known and widely sold soon after the turn of the century under the name of Arthur's Club Mixture.

Redolent of 'richly scented snuff', with an 'atmosphere like that of a perfumer's shop', is Macaulay's description of the coffee-houses. The same words without exaggeration might well have been employed to describe the clubs that succeeded the coffee-houses, and indeed would have fitted as well almost any other gathering places or scenes of social meeting in the Britain of the eighteenth century. Beyond the London which provides most of our glimpses of snuff-taking history, snuff was as prominent in the life of the time all over England, Scotland, Ireland and Wales. Authoritative, if brief, reminders of the part played by snuff in serious affairs as well as in social life come from

III Snuff-shop interior showing earthenware storage jars

IV Lead Canister, Glass Jar and Pottery Jars, in which superior snuffs were sold

varied sources. Talleyrand, master of diplomacy and hardened snuffer, who came to England in 1791 and later appeared as Ambassador in London, spoke of snuff as indispensable in his calling, in that the opening of his snuff-box and the taking of a pinch allowed him time to think out an answer to an awkward question or conceal his reaction to an adversary's statement. Scott, making many references to snuff and snuff-takers in the Waverley Novels, confirmed the Scotsman's reputation for 'enriching his nose'[1] lavishly and frequently from his mull; and it was the opinion of another undoubted Scotsman, Dugald Stewart (quoted by more than one later authority on the subject), that snuff civilized Scotland and was responsible for the country's great men of the eighteenth century. On the world at large, according to the same authority, snuff had an incalculably improving influence, making it 'more humane and even-tempered. . . . Had the western hemisphere discovered the tobacco plant earlier, historians would have had much more pleasant events to chronicle. It is most probable that the fate of Rome, discussed by a triumvirate over their snuff-boxes, would have been different'.

Allusions in verse to snuff-taking continued to appear throughout the eighteenth century. To the few already quoted should be added the feelings expressed in two lines by the gentle poet Cowper, who found that snuff

> Does thought more quicken and refine
> Than all the breath of all the Nine.

Of another order of poetry were the verses giving one answer to several questions:

> What introduces Whig and Tory,
> And reconciles them in their story,
> When each is boasting in his glory?
> A pinch of snuff!

[1] 'I will enrich thy nose with snuff from my mull'.—*Heart of Midlothian*.

> Where speech and tongue together fail
> What helps old ladies in their tale,
> And adds fresh canvas to their sail?
>   A pinch of snuff!

Nor was snuff forgotten by the punster-rhymster school:

> Knows he that never took a pinch—
> Nosey—the pleasure thence that flows?
> Knows he the titillating joy
> Which my nose knows?
> Oh Nose! I am as proud of thee
> As a mountain of its snows.
> I gaze on thee and feel the pride
>   A Roman knows.

Opponents and detractors of snuff-taking remained well represented at the end of the century, though less numerous and noisy than they had been in earlier years. One of them was that fashionable celebrity Doctor Abernethy. His verdict on snuff became an oft-repeated *bon mot* which added considerably to his reputation as a wit; it was given in the first place in answer to a patient's question.

'Pray, Doctor,' said the patient, 'is snuff harmful to the brain?'

'That it cannot be,' replied Abernethy, 'since nobody possessing any brain would dream of taking it.'

CHAPTER III

Snuff-taking after the Eighteenth Century

FOREMOST among historic and colourful figures of the first part of the nineteenth century were distinguished snuff-takers. Pursuit of the more entertaining snuff associations from the year 1800 inevitably leads to the fourth George, a devotee of snuff throughout his life as Prince of Wales, Regent and King; to his mother, Queen Charlotte, whose love of her snuff-box earned her in later life the nickname of 'Snuffy Charlotte'; and to certain confirmed and faithful snuffers among their most picturesque subjects.

The first years of the new century saw snuff keeping its popularity in high places, notwithstanding symptoms of a return to smoking by men. Already well known in America and Spain, the 'segar' was making its appearance in Britain with all the attractions of a novelty to recommend it to fashionable youth: pipe-smoking was becoming much more usual than had been the case a few years earlier, with soldiers, sailors and at least one of George III's sons setting an example in taking to the habit. But snuff remained the fashion; a fashion set at Court, at Carlton House, at the Royal Pavilion at Brighton, in the clubs of St. James's, and followed by almost everyone of any social standing or pretensions. If the period was the last in which snuff thus reigned supreme in the world of fashion and culture, it was perhaps the richest in snuff-taking celebrities and associations; a period in which snuff was not only taken in quantities that now seem fabulous, but was studied by many of its takers to the extent of originating private

51

blends of their own, taking different blends at given hours
of the day with separate mixtures for morning, afternoon
and evening, and amassing hoards or collections of snuff
in much the same way as cellars of wine were laid down.

It is in recording the custom of historically or socially
significant snuff-takers of this time that the business
records of Fribourg & Treyer have most interest and
value. Without a dull page the firm's day books and
ledgers set out in detail from the beginning of the nineteenth century the orders of members of Royal and noble
houses, of dignitaries of Church and State, soldiers,
sailors, actors, actresses, artists, authors, sporting squires,
beaux, and men and women in nearly every walk of life
that gave distinction to the age, with the kinds and quantities of snuff that were their preferences; until at length,
in the reign of Queen Victoria, snuff orders become
fewer, and eventually are almost lost among those for
cigars and smoking tobacco.

The name of George, Prince of Wales, afterwards
George IV, appears for the first time in the day books of
1799. In the following year and thereafter his snuff orders
were of frequent occurrence. As in other matters, his
taste in snuff was versatile; a fact borne out by the
number of imported kinds and blends supplied to him
over a period of years. Under the heading 'His Royal
Highness the Prince of Wales' one of his first purchases
in the new century was noted on 25 October 1800; '¼ lb.
Morlaix & Cannister, ¾ lb. Seville & Do. (By Chairman).'
At about the same time he was buying some of 'Mr.
Colling Smith's sort', this being one of the many blends
always referred to in the accounts as 'sorts', which were
mixed by the firm to conform to the exact stipulations of
clients who found satisfaction only in a precisely propor-
tioned blend of several varieties of snuff. Evidently a
pinch accepted on some social occasion from Mr. Colling
Smith's box, filled with his personal choice, had pleased

the Prince and had led to an order to his suppliers. Within a month another private sort—no less than twelve pounds of it—was entered in the Prince's account: this was Lord Ed. Bentinck's blend, duly noted with '2 Jars & Bung, 4d.' The custom of Lord Edward Bentinck himself is shown elsewhere in the same book, together with a memorandum of his calling personally to discharge a debt for 'freight and Postage and wharfage of a Jar and Box'.

Yet sold by the firm is a scented blend, based on Black Rappee of medium coarse grain, which bears the name of Prince's Mixture and commemorates the Regent's preference at one time for a snuff less apt than the lighter coloured fine ground varieties to soil a dark coat, if a few grains should be dropped on it. His tastes in snuff, however, changed as often as his taste in coats, and throughout his life he continued to experiment with new ideas in snuff character and flavouring. Like many other hardened snuffers of his age, he would use different snuffs at the different hours of the day, finding one blend a suitable stimulant to the duties of the morning, while another was worked out especially to accompany the day's close. The King's Morning Mixture and the King's Evening Mixture were both among the blends supplied to him by the Haymarket firm in the years that followed his accession to the throne.

In 1802, according to the books, Strasbourg snuff had become the Prince's choice of the moment, a pound of it being despatched to the Royal Pavilion at Brighton on 31 July, and a note being made of a charge of eightpence for 'Cannister and booking'. By January, 1812—his orders now booked under the heading 'H.R.H. the Prince Regent'—he was ordering Masulipatam, at a guinea the bottle, together with '5 Samples' (unspecified) at 6s. 3d. A fortnight later the account was continued with an order for Colonel Taylor's sort, 4 lb. of it in a jar, and at about this time a note appears of the receipt of a cash payment of £33 7s. 9d. in part settlement of the bill, amounting in all to £36 13s. 0d.

It seems possible that Queen Charlotte may have introduced to her son some of the snuffs for which his orders show a preference, and this is most likely to have been so in the case of the last one noted, the Queen's account in the same book including an earlier entry of '6 lb. Col. Taylor's, strong with Masm.' (Masulipatam), and another a little later for a bottle of Masulipatam at a guinea. Her account with the firm was an old and valued one. Entries under the simple heading 'Her Majesty' are many and her requests for the supply of 'Marrocca' remained consistent over a considerable period. For 20 February 1804 we may read:

Her Majesty.	10 lb. Marrocca, at 8s. 6d.	£4	5s.	0d.
	Jar & Bung.		4s.	0d.
	2 lb. Do.		17s.	0d.
May, 26th.	6 lb. Do.	2	11s.	0d.

Repeated deliveries of Morocco follow, changing on occasion to Colonel Taylor's or Masulipatam as from time to time the account was presented to and promptly discharged by the Queen's agent, Mr. Compton of Charlotte Street, Pimlico.

If the quantities of snuff supplied in this case seem generous when read of in an age when snuff-takers commonly fulfil their wants with purchases of an ounce or less—and many buy no more than a quarter of an ounce at a time as being enough to fill an average snuff-box of waistcoat pocket dimensions—they serve to substantiate the Queen's reputation for drawing comfort from her snuff-box at intervals both regular and frequent. Contradictory opinions on her love of snuff have been left to history, varying from praise of the neat elegance with which she was said to handle her snuff-box to the condemnation of the few who gave her the nickname of

'Snuffy Charlotte' and showed their dislike of the traces and odour of the habit which they professed to notice about her person.

Though it is assumed that the Queen's snuff orders were intended to supply her current needs and perhaps those of some of her household, some of the quantities which her son, the Prince, continued to buy may have had another purpose than immediate use. For many years as Regent and King he added to and built up a private store of snuff, which he put by as though he were laying down a cellar of wine for the consumption of another generation. At length this Royal collection of snuffs came to fill an entire room at Windsor, and by the time of its owner's death had reached such proportions that it had to be disposed of by sale, much of it returning once more to the trade.

The Princess Charlotte, the Regent's unhappy daughter, and his brother, the Duke of Sussex, were other members of the Royal House whose service is shown in these day books. During the girlhood of the Princess her repeated purchases of *Bureau*, a modest quarter pound at a time, costing half-a-crown, were bought perhaps to fill a box for the use of her visitors and staff.[1] Under the heading '1805. H.R.H. the Duke of Sussex' is shown a charge of 17s. 4d. for '2 lb. Dr. Ruddiman's in canister'. Thereafter the evidence convicts the Duke, alone among his family, of having been a smoker as well as a snuffer: as both, his needs were supplied; '6 Pipes and Box full Etrennes, 1s. 9d.'; later, '¼ lb. Latakia', and more, and yet more pipes. *Etrennes* denotes the snuff long before distinguished by having been the choice of Horace Walpole, and Latakia a pipe tobacco in later years to be much used in blended smoking mixtures; the pipes of course were clays.

---

[1] The entries are headed 'H.R.H. Princess Charlotte'; it is assumed that they refer to the Prince Regent's daughter, though the client may have been Charlotte, Princess Royal, eldest daughter of George III and Queen Charlotte.

Other sales to smokers at this period show that, however slightly, the sovereignty of snuff was declining. Many such entries bear earlier dates and concern the 'segars' and cheroots that appeared so long before the Havana cigar was known in England. One item of this kind may be noted as disclosing the identity of an early convert to the new cult: 'Oct. 8th., 1802. The Duke of Manchester, Cheroots. £1. 1. 0.'

Symptoms of the slow but inevitable return to smoking for years were few and inconspicuous. Snuff retained the affection of the majority of men and women in the walks of life catered for by Fribourg & Treyer, and the old ledgers show how diverse were the lives and callings of these clients. To represent the Church, one could select from many entries the Bishop of Ely, in 1803 and thereabouts buying his 'Paris C.' (coarse), in quantities of from two to six pounds at a time; or 'the Hon. Ed. Legge, the Revd. the Dean of Windsor', with his marked liking for *Bureau Gros* and *Étrennes Fin*, blended half and half. In the Army one need go no farther than the 'Hon. Mr. Wellesley', before he became Sir Arthur and when the dukedom of Wellington and the Battle of Waterloo still lay years ahead, ordering first that same 'Honble. E. Legge's sort' and then a quarter pound of *Étrennes* alone. At sea, Captain Hardy, of Nelson fame, aboard the *Vanguard* was using a snuff which the firm were called upon to supply again more than a century and a quarter later to fill Hardy's snuff-box, then presented to the modern *Vanguard*. From the theatre, between 1804 and 1811, came Mrs. Siddons, of 49, Great Marlborough Street, to buy her snuff from the same shop that Garrick had dealt with in earlier years; and entries of 1803 remind us that 'Mr. Reeve, the Stage Door Keeper, Haymarket Theatre', regularly walked up the street for his pound or half pound of fine *Bureau*. The worlds of politics, art and literature are well represented, even better so the field of sport and the ranks of country gentlemen. Of racing men of fame there were several to succeed Major St. Leger, who as far back as in 1766 opened an account for snuff (which amounted to £8 11s. 7d.), ten years before his name was given to the oldest of the Classic races, run for the first time in 1776 and then won by Allabaculia. Hunting field associations cling to the Duke of Beaufort, who carried Bolangaro in his snuff-box, and to 'Mr. Ashton Smith'. The latter was Thomas Assheton Smith, perhaps the hardest-riding man in hunting history, of whom it was said that he had fallen in every field in Leicestershire and once had encouraged a friend out with the Quorn by remarking, 'There is no place in this country that cannot be got over *with a fall*'. His preference in snuff was an unusual one, for Coarse Irish. This he was buying in the Haymarket at least seven years before he took over the Mastership of the Quorn Hunt, an office in which he was succeeded by the equally famous Squire Osbaldeston.

George IV himself would be as hard to imagine without snuff as would George Bryan Brummell during the years he held his place in the Prince's favour and in the social life of St. James's and Brighton. Though never a taker of snuff in the excessive quantities of some of his generation, Beau Brummell used it consistently throughout his life, treating fine snuffs and fine snuff-boxes as things of the first importance, and selecting and buying both with the same studied care he gave to clothes and personal adornment. To be a connoisseur of snuff was as essential in an arbiter of elegance and fashion as to know more than other men about matters sartorial; Brummell accordingly made himself a snuff authority.

At the peak of his social eminence he was followed as slavishly in his choice of snuff as in his verdicts on the folding of a stock, the sit of a coat or the polish of a boot: a few words from him could as easily mar as make the sales of a snuff blend fresh to the London market. On

E

one famous occasion his usually prompt sources of information had been a little late in letting him know of the arrival of a consignment of Martinique, imported by Fribourg & Treyer. He reached the Haymarket in time to find already present in the shop a gathering of his acquaintances, who had marked their approval of the snuff by reserving for their own use the whole of the quantity available. Equal to the occasion, as ever, Brummell helped himself to a pinch, made a wry face and condemned the delightful snuff as being of inferior quality and altogether beneath the attention of a gentleman. In the face of this verdict the would-be connoisseurs dissembled their feelings, withdrew their orders for the Martinique and departed. Brummell then made clear to the importer his true assessment of the snuff's high value and placed an order for several jars of it for his own use, apologizing for having omitted to do so before. The rest of the consignment, he implied, would find a ready market at almost any price as a snuff distinguished by the unqualified approval of Mr. Brummell; and later events were to prove his forecast correct.

The annals of Brummell's years of privilege and brilliance, when the Prince deferred to him, social England was at his feet and sufficient means kept insolvency at bay, contain many references to the part played in his life by snuff and snuff-boxes. Handsome and expensive snuff-boxes he acquired until he had formed a collection of them to equal that long before built up by Beau Nash at Bath. Some lavishly ornamented and extremely costly, others quaint or unique from some unusual feature, but all elegant and exhibiting their owner's taste, Brummell's boxes were among his particular prides. Together they were shown to visitors at his London home, and singly those intended for the pocket were each used in turn. One to which he was deeply attached was a gold box which closed with a secret fastening known only to its owner and effectually reserving its contents for his own use and that of the few among his acquaintance to whom he thought a pinch might be offered without loss of dignity to himself. While staying at Belvoir Castle on one occasion, Brummell was one of many guests at dinner; the lavish meal was ending and snuff-boxes were being produced, the Beau's unusual box attracting the attention of his immediate neighbours at table, none of whom were able to open it. Passed from hand to hand, it reached at length a gentleman who attempted to prize open the lid with a dessert knife. With perfect self-possession which concealed his annoyance at this maltreatment of his treasured box, Brummell turned to his host with a request: 'Perhaps, Sir, you will be kind enough to remind your friend that my snuff-box is not an oyster.'

Another dining occasion was one at the Royal Pavilion at Brighton: George, Prince of Wales, was entertaining a company of the first distinction and, as so often, George Brummell was among his guests, another of whom was the Bishop of Winchester. The Beau's snuff-box lay open on the table before him when, without invitation, the Bishop helped himself to a generous pinch from it. Turning to the servant who stood behind his chair, Brummell ordered the man in audible tones to remove the defiled box, throw away its contents and fill it with fresh snuff. Later the Prince, who had angrily observed the whole affair, privately reprimanded Brummell, and is said never to have forgotten or forgiven the studied insult to the Bishop.

At least one writer of fiction dealing with this period has adapted a Brummell snuff story to suit a fictitious character, and Conan Doyle's Sir Charles Tregellis it was who compared the sacredness of a man's bestowal of the freedom to take a pinch from his snuff-box with that of a woman's gift of her affections, limiting those who were made free of his own box to the Prince of Wales, the

French Ambassador and one privileged Peer of the
Realm. It was an Irish bishop who in this case sullied a
snuff-box by dipping into it an uninvited finger and
thumb.

Of the several incidents which culminated in Brummell's losing the Prince's friendship and favour, and the
eventual tragic flight to France of the debtor who for so
long had held an unchallenged and unequalled position
in society, one of the first was the affair of the snuff-box
soiled by the touch of a bishop. Another of the Beau's
snuff-boxes had a later and more prominent place in the
story of his downfall. The box was one of considerable
value and great beauty which had attracted the attention
of the Prince, taking his fancy to an extent that only its
possession would satisfy. Some of the historians who
have remembered the occasion when it passed from
Brummell's ownership to that of the Prince Regent recall
the latter's exact words: 'Brummell, this box must be
mine! Go to Gray's and order any box you like to take
its place.' Thus instructed, the Beau amused himself by
drawing up an elaborate design for the box with which
he was to be compensated, flattering the Regent by insist-
ing that a portrait of him should be framed in its lid and
receiving his assent to the extravagance of having the
miniature set round with diamonds. Craftsmen began
work on it at once, the Prince even inspecting the miniature portrait in its early stages and suggesting certain
improvements. Before the work had advanced much
farther, however, several misfortunes had befallen Brummell, among them his ill-judged reference to Mrs. Fitz-
herbert. His friendship with the Prince had become a
thing of the past by the time it occurred to him to call at
Gray's for the box: arrived at the shop, he received,
instead of the valuable gift he had been promised, a curt
intimation that the order had been cancelled on the
instructions of the Prince Regent.

Brummell left England for France in May, 1816, and never returned. Among the effects he left behind him was a snuff-box that provided a dramatic moment at the sale held on behalf of his creditors. Christie, the auctioneer, was inviting bids for the box when he opened its lid; from within fell a scrap of paper on which the Beau had written, 'This snuff-box was intended for the Prince Regent if he had conducted himself with more propriety toward me.'

Various entries in the Fribourg & Treyer books record the custom of Beau Brummell during his years in London, and that of his elder brother William, who lived in Essex. The Beau's orders were seldom for more than moderate quantities of snuff, and in view of all that has been chronicled and said of the mass of debts he left behind him in the West End it is interesting to note that his account with this firm was settled with regularity until within a year of his departure for France. The amount he owed thereafter was less than £16, which remained unpaid at the time of his death. A part of this figure no doubt was accounted for by nominal charges made without much expectation of their being paid for snuff sent to him during his years of indigence abroad. It is not very difficult to guess that at this time occasional supplies of favourite blends were forwarded by his old purveyors as a kindly token of remembrance of other days rather than as business transactions, notwithstanding any rash promises contained in the last letter received from Brummell. Framed and treasured, as it deserves to be, by the firm to whom it was addressed, this letter reads:

Calais, May 28.

Mr. Brummell is very much obliged to Messrs. Fribourg and Treyer for the snuff they have had the goodness to send him—it is excellent, and he will consider it a particular favour if they will from time to time, when they have any really good Martinique or Façon de Paris, remit him a certain quantity not exceeding 2½ lb. at a time, directed for him to the care of M. Quillacq, Dessein's Hotel, Calais, and he will immediately upon the receipt send them an order for payment.

Mr. Brummell begs to assure Messrs. Fribourg and Treyer that their recollection of him is not less seasonable than flattering, for there is not a good pinch of snuff to be had throughout France.

The quickest as well as the most secure conveyance from London to this place is from the Black Bear in Piccadilly.

Written in the neat handwriting of a man who studied neatness in everything he did, the letter suggests something of Brummell's character. The dignified address in the third person is that of one still conscious of his importance; the well-turned phrases and the hint of fun are those of the master of the apt remark; the touch of flattery is sufficient without being over-done, and typical is the wholesale condemnation of all the snuff in France and the gloriously illogical request that one French snuff and one coming from a French possession should be supplied from England. The absence of a complete date leaves an uncertainty as to the year in which the letter was written; perhaps it was sent in the first summer the Beau spent abroad, in which case it was one of his earliest communications with London after an absence of a few days; but more probably it belongs to a year or two later. It was to Dessein's Hotel, the haven of so many English refugees from debt, that he went on his first arrival, staying there for only a short while but continuing to make much use of the place and its accommodating owner, Monsieur Quillacq, even after a more permanent home had been found in rooms above a Calais bookshop. One of Brummell's first actions on reaching France was to sell to Quillacq the travelling carriage for which he was to have no further use. Settled in his rooms, he overlooked nothing which could help him to feel at home in a foreign land, and such snuff-boxes as he had brought with him from England were at once set out on the central table of his sitting-room. When, very soon afterwards, he felt the need of a new toy, he gratified the want at once by ordering from a local craftsman an elaborate snuff-box of gold and dark tortoise-shell, without giving a thought to its cost or the means of paying for it.

Constantly did snuff and snuff-boxes continue to play their part in the remaining years of Brummell's life, both during and after the long and uneasy time he spent in Calais, living in the hope of an appointment to a British consulship or vice-consulship in a French town. When at last, after George IV's death, such a position was granted him in Caen, he celebrated his new dignity with an extravagant week's stay in Paris, there making the acquaintance of that very snuffy diplomat Talleyrand, and spending a great deal of time in searching the jewellers' shops of the Rue de la Paix for a snuff-box that should be worthy in its magnificence of his freshly acquired importance. It seems that Paris could not produce such a box ready made, so one was ordered from Dabert's, to be copied in gold and enamels from a pattern provided by the Beau. Its price was 450 francs, the equivalent of his expectations of income for almost three months ahead. Later came the calamity which Brummell had left England to avoid; imprisoned for debt in Caen, he found himself in surroundings which to him were peculiarly squalid and fearful, cut off from all the minor luxuries he had been able to cling to so far. A friend was summoned and promptly despatched to the Beau's lodgings to fetch a supply of immediate necessities, among which were several changes of pantaloons, shirts and waistcoats, some bottles of toilet preparations and oil for his wig, and—particularly specified—a glass jar of Macouba snuff.

The last melancholy chapters of Brummell's life tell of his admission to the Bon Saveur, a Caen asylum, and of his death there in 1840. Not long before this had been a wretched period of poverty in which the broken man had parted with the last of his possessions and trinkets of any value, one of them his only remaining silver snuff-box.

Had the unhappy Beau been as moderate in all things—particularly in gambling and in his choice of remarks about influential personages—as he was in his use of snuff, his career might have been a very different one, closing perhaps as brilliantly as it had opened. As his purchases in the Haymarket show, he was not a heavy snuffer in the way that some of his contemporaries were; the particular snuff-taking reputation which will always cling to his name was based on his critical taste in good snuffs, his dilettante interest in snuff-boxes of fine manufacture and his emphasised elegance in the act of taking snuff. This last was a planned and practised succession of graceful movements beginning with his production of the box from his pocket, followed by a dexterous opening of the box with the same hand in which it was held—the left; and ending with a carefully judged, but not over-elaborate or theatrical, gesture with the right arm as the finger and thumb of the right hand raised to the nostrils a pinch from which not one grain was allowed to fall.

One who in Brummell's time shared many of his tastes, carrying some of them to extremes of eccentricity, was Lord Petersham. In the niceties of dress Petersham never reached the Beau's perfection, though an acknowledged dandy and the originator of the 'Petersham Coat', one of the sartorial triumphs of the age. Worshipping smartness as did Brummel, Petersham yet went a little beyond the bounds of discretion and good taste as Brummell defined them. Though immaculate, Petersham's clothes were rather too ostentatious, and the same tendency to exaggerate distinguished him in all things. The spotless curricle which he delighted in driving at a time when he was enamoured of a lady named Mrs Brown was painted brown, drawn by brown horses in brown harness and attended by a groom in brown livery. When Petersham

V A part of Queen Charlotte's snuff account—ledger extract,
1799–1803

VI Old snuff-seller's rasp (*above*). Sieving snuff in the present day (*below*)

developed a fondness for tea-drinking he set himself to build up a store of tea which would have stocked several shops, hoarding away countless canisters of Souchong, Gunpowder and Pekoe for his own and his guests' use. It was the same with snuff, and with snuff-boxes: he collected both with a whole-hearted enthusiasm giving him a place in the first rank of notable snuff-takers.

Judged on the quantities of snuff he bought, Lord Petersham could be counted the greatest of all English snuffers. Constantly dealing with Fribourg & Treyer over a long period, he probably took up more space in their day books than any other customer, and certainly no other placed his orders on such a scale. In 1809, for example, when the building up of his great collection of snuffs was receiving his earnest attention, we find under his name an entry for 7 December showing that he bought 48 lb. of Bordeaux at 9s. the pound. This is followed by notes of charges for five jars and corks, a credit for the return of two jars, and evidence of purchases of Martinique. To deal with his private stock of snuff and the blending operations he appeared to be carrying on at home he had recourse to the services of the firm's staff, as is shown by the next entry: '2 men sifting Quantity of snuff, and a scoop.' The same account follows on in January 1810 with: '13 lb Old Etrennes, 13 lb Bordeaux, 4 lb Spanish Bran . . .' and so on until, with '4 lb Domingo' his Lordship was presented with a bill for £77 1s. 9d.

This kind of thing went on at intervals for years, the relations between client and firm being always of a personal and friendly character commemorated by several exchanges of courtesy. On one occasion Lord Petersham decided that he had bought rather more of certain snuffs than his requirements justified and suggested sending some back to the firm, who promptly accepted the return of *two hundred and sixteen pounds* of snuff and credited his

Lordship's account with £75 12s. At another time one of
the partners in the business received, by way of a token
of appreciation of continued service, an amboyna wood
snuff-box, lined with gold; still to be seen, it is inscribed
within the lid: 'Presented to George Evans by Lord
Petersham, 1819'.

For at least a quarter of a century, possibly for very
much longer, Lord Petersham followed his hobby of
collecting snuff, acquiring only imported varieties of the
highest repute, in most cases owing their fragrances to
fine tobaccos blended in carefully measured proportions
rather than to the addition of scents or essences. The
only comparable rival to his collection in either quality
or quantity was the one housed in Windsor Castle and
formed on similar principles over so many years by
George IV, and a considerable part of that was to find
its way eventually to the Petersham hoard. When in
1830, after the King's death, the Royal snuff was disposed
of, Fribourg & Treyer were the buyers of large quantities both on their own account and at the behest of
the Earl of Harrington, as Lord Petersham had become
by that time. Duly noted in the books are the snuffs
selected for his collection on this occasion, with their
quantities and prices:

18 lbs. Old Bureau (1801)	£13 17s.	0d.
18 lbs. Old Cologne (1818)	13 17s.	0d.
18 lbs. Old Arras (1818)	13 17s.	0d.
12 lbs. Old Havre (1815)	9 6s.	0d.
18 lbs. Bureau Demi-gros	13 17s.	0d.
6 lbs. French Prize (1810)	4 13s.	6d.
1 lb. French Prize	16s.	0d.
5 lbs. Old Rouen (1801)	3 17s.	6d.

The dates appended to most of the snuffs denote the
years in which the King had bought them, their maturity
having earned them also the prefix Old; almost certainly
they were perfection from the connoisseur's point of

view, age having had much the same mellowing and improving effect as it has upon wine.

In his collecting of snuff-boxes Petersham was as wholesale as he was in his laying by of snuff. In numbers his boxes totalled many hundreds, and all were used in turn, his method being to select each day from the collection a box which he deemed peculiarly suitable to that particular day's character, the company in which it was to be spent, or the weather, and to carry the box for that day only. The following morning another box would be chosen and filled with whatever blend happened to be his fancy of the moment, and so on throughout the year, it being a rule that no box should be used more than once in twelve months. When three hundred and sixty-five boxes had been given an airing in turn it was permissible to repeat their use, though the immensity of the collection did not by any means confine the owner's selections within that number.

It was Lord Petersham who was said to have caught a bad cold on one occasion through leaving the choice of a snuff-box to his valet instead of, as was his wont, attending to the important matter himself. The day in question was a winter's one with a keen wind blowing, to which perhaps a stout horn or tortoise-shell box might have been appropriate, but thoughtlessly the servant allowed his master to go out with no better protection than a little filigree-adorned trifle of egg-shell thickness and intended only to be used at midsummer. If not strictly true, the story at all events was widely circulated, and it is possible to imagine Lord Petersham himself making the best use of it to advance the eccentric reputation which it amused him to cultivate.

Less generally associated with snuff-taking than such men as Brummell and Petersham were certain notabilities of the same period whose use of snuff is disclosed by the Fribourg & Treyer books. Some of the names occurring in the day books covering the first forty years or so of the nineteenth century were entered at a time when as names they meant little and in fact were nearly unknown to the world at large, though later history was to give them importance and interest. One such name is that of 'D'Israeli, Esqre.', appearing, from 1826 to 1827, as a purchaser of a blend of three-fourths Amsterdam *Fin* and one fourth Amsterdam Round Grain. Then in his early twenties, the future Earl of Beaconsfield had been but a short while entered at Lincoln's Inn and was busy with the publication of *Vivian Grey*, his first literary achievement. Ten years were yet to elapse before he entered parliament after three unsuccessful attempts at election; another ten before he became the virtual leader of his party; and twenty more before he succeeded Lord Derby as head of the administration. When he proclaimed Queen Victoria Empress of India, and thereafter took his seat in the House of Lords as Earl of Beaconsfield, almost exactly half a century had elapsed from the time of his qualifying as a customer for snuff in the Haymarket.

Side by side with men who took snuff before they made English history appear as many who belonged to other countries but bought their snuff in England. One entry which perhaps might be held to endorse Brummell's opinion of French snuff unless it was bought in London, was made in 1819. On May 11th of that year fifty pounds of *Carotte Bureau*, at half a guinea the pound, was despatched, especially packed in '23 flat canisters', to the order of King Louis XVIII of France. Eighteen years later the Russian Ambassador was shown to have developed a taste for a fifty-fifty blend of Martinique and *Bureau Fin*, which he required delivered to No. 30, Dover Street. Another volume, known as the Export Book, gives details of the considerable quantities of snuff sent between the years 1800 and 1811 to clients abroad. In this are shown exports to diverse parts of the world, including

Madeira, Calcutta, various parts of America, both East and West Indies, Gibraltar, Malta, and such European cities as Lisbon, Frankfort and St. Petersburg. Among these places it is illuminating to read the names of several which were, or had been, themselves famous as sources of snuffs of high reputation, notably Lisbon and Frankfort. A wider interest than that of snuff belongs to one entry showing St. Helena to have been the destination of a parcel made up of 'Best Black, Best Brown and Best Scotch', packed together with fifty-four Tonquin beans for flavouring in lead canisters, and consigned by permit to a certain Mrs Hastier, and others who are assumed to have been members of an island garrison. Bearing a date in 1810, this shipment might perhaps have been allowed another significance if it had been sent some five years later, when that confirmed snuff-taker Napoleon landed on the island where his last years were to be spent. The last of all the export items recorded is that of some snuff sent to Malta in 1811 for the use of a Mr James Cowper, whose address is given as Ely Place, at the request of Messrs. Lundy Foot and Company. Though the way in which the name of the famous Dublin snuff firm was noted does not make clear their part in the transaction, it is fair to conclude that the order was one given to them by a former Dublin resident but which they handed on to their agents in the Haymarket.[1]

One more of the Treyer books must be remembered. It is that in which notes were made of customers' private 'sorts' or blends, with the kinds and proportions of the snuffs which went to their mixing. Endless varieties of flavour are suggested by page after page of the recipes of snuff-takers of exacting and particular tastes, whose orders for a supply of 'the mixture as before' were

---

[1] On a Fribourg & Treyer label printed at about this time appears: 'Exporter of Foreign Snuffs and Tobaccos', and also 'Lundy Foot's High Dried Irish Snuffs'.

promptly fulfilled by reference to this volume. Again, as in the ledgers and day books, a long period is covered by the entries and many names of historical or snuffy significance make their appearance. A random choice made from the earlier pages provides the blend liked in 1807 by 'W. Brummell, Esqre.', the Beau's elder brother: '$\frac{1}{4}$ Bureau fin, $\frac{1}{4}$ Etrennes fin, $\frac{1}{4}$ Longueville, $\frac{1}{4}$ Abbeville'. As an alternative the same client used a mixture of equal parts Morlaix, *Bureau* and Morocco. Covering the Regency and the reigns of George IV and William IV are countless entries giving the 'sorts' devised by men and woman whose snuff tastes have been remembered earlier in this chapter; while later, within the reign of Queen Victoria, come others to prove the survival of the exacting connoisseur of snuff despite steadily increasing numbers of smokers. The Duke of Buccleuch recorded in 1843 his 'new mixture' of half Old Paris and half Frankfort, superseding the equal proportions of Bolongaro and Port au Prince which he gave as his preference two years earlier. The Marquis of Ely, who as Lord Loftus had been a buyer of Virginia *Carotte* and Mixed *Carotte* as far back as in 1802, blossomed out in the eighteen-forties with so many ingenious and oft-changed combinations of foreign snuffs that several pages and insertions were needed to register his changes of mind. His appearances in the Haymarket at this time almost invariably signalised the announcement of a new discovery and the dictation of a fresh entry in the recipe book. From '$\frac{1}{4}$ St. Vincent, $\frac{1}{4}$ Mannheim, $\frac{1}{2}$ French Carotte', to '$\frac{1}{4}$ Vincent gros, $\frac{1}{4}$ Bureau gros, $\frac{1}{2}$ Old Paris' was his first change in his most active period, beginning in 1840. By 1844 some seven or more of the Marquis's further inspirations had been noted, the one referred to as his 'Fourth Mixture' remaining perhaps the most memorable with its five components, the first of which was one of the historic snuffs acquired fourteen years earlier from

George IV's collection at Windsor: '¼ King's Carotte, ¼ Dieppe, ¼ Cologne, ¼ Etrennes gros with a little Brazil'.

The last dates mentioned belong to a period in which snuff-taking had lost what W. A. Penn describes as its fashionability. 1825 is the date selected by this authority as the turning point, when snuff's social importance became noticeably less; certainly the opening of Queen Victoria's reign—when so many fashions and established habits were uprooted—saw snuff surviving mainly in changed social surroundings. At this time historians who made any mention at all of snuffing could find none of the entertainment and anecdote of a little earlier to associate with the habit, and began to allude to it as a middle-class practice considered respectable in circles which condemned smoking. Besant, writing of the year of the Queen's accession, 1837, states that: 'Tobacco was not admitted in any shape except that of snuff into the better kind of middle-class house; only working men smoked vulgar pipes'. Nevertheless it was smoking that was supplanting snuffing at the top as well as elsewhere in the social scale. Buyers of snuff noted in diminishing numbers in the Haymarket books were mainly elder men surviving from the Georgian age into the Victorian. Havana cigars were finding a wider market, some of the leading brands becoming known by name. An expensive and refined alternative to the clay had appeared in the form of the meerschaum pipe, and younger men found a new diversion in colouring their meerschaums slowly and systematically from virgin waxed whiteness to rich mahogany, even if their smoking indoors was permitted only in privacy or in the kitchen. Women so far had found no alternative to snuff, but snuffing no longer was considered a ladylike accomplishment.

Cigar Divans became a feature of Town life at this period, and some snuffy as well as smoking associations belong to them. Since they sold the materials for smoking and snuffing they were in a sense tobacconists shops, but for the men-about-town who frequented them they also provided comfortably-furnished apartments for the 'on the premises' consumption of their wares and served such refreshments as coffee to their customers, thus inheriting a little of the character of the old coffee-houses. Within the lounge-like premises of a Cigar Divan a man of leisure— debarred from polluting the atmosphere of his home with tobacco smoke—could smoke himself sick and put into practice all the twelve rules for 'the right smoking of a cigar' which a writer of 1829 found it necessary to lay down in print. He could also enjoy the society and conversation of kindred spirits in surroundings more exotic and carefree than those of his club, his refreshments being served the while on a table which bore also current newspapers and light reading. According to Besant, Cigar Divans in 1837 were 'as yet only one or two' in London; but one of the most celebrated—Gliddon's—is noted in Hone's *Table Book* as having been open for business in 1826. To be found in King Street, Gliddon's Cigar Divan was a pattern of its kind. Luxuriously furnished within, the smoking-room aped the appearance of the temporary abode of an Eastern potentate, its walls and ceiling being draped in the manner of a large tent while the customers could recline on gaudily upholstered divans. Cigars, hookahs, pipes and varied tobaccos were provided for smokers by the enterprising Mr. Gliddon, who also stocked for his more conservative clients a selection of fine snuffs. Snuff and certain philosophic reflections on its value figure largely in a conversation retailed by Hone as having been overheard in Gliddon's Divan, those taking part being the proprietor and two of his customers:

C.—'Some snuff, however.'
Mr. Gliddon.—'The best to be had.'
W.—'Take some of mine; I have cropped the flower of the shop.'

C.—'Snuff's a capital thing! I cannot help thinking there is something providential in snuff. If you observe, different refreshments come up among nations at different eras of the world. In the Elizabethan age it was beef-steaks. Then tea and coffee came up; and people being irritable sometimes, perhaps with the new light let in upon them by the growth of the press, snuff was sent us to support uneasy thoughts.'

Fiction is more helpful than history at this period in revealing the social place of snuffing and the gradual acceptance of smoking. Dickens, always noting precisely the habits of his characters, sprinkled the pages of *Pickwick Papers* with snuff-takers and smokers whose ages and positions in life are significant of the trend of the time. Appearing early in the chronicle of Mr. Pickwick's travels and adventures are two snuffers of the old school: 'Colonel Bulder and Sir Thomas Clubber exchanged snuff-boxes, and looked very much like a pair of Alexander Selkirks: "Monarchs of all they surveyed" '. The Colonel and Sir Thomas are both elderly and representative of the already declining number of snuff-takers of the upper class. Dickens, who almost invariably caricatured his social superiors, indulged only in a comparatively mild gibe at the well born in this case while making clear the fine-drawn class distinctions at a provincial gathering: 'While the aristocracy of the place—the Bulders, and Clubbers, and Snipes—were thus preserving their dignity at the upper end of the room, the other classes of society were imitating their example in other parts of it. The less aristocratic officers of the 97th devoted themselves to the families of the less important functionaries of the dock yard . . .', and so on down the scale.

Within a paragraph or so snuff is introduced again in slightly humbler circumstances: 'Doctor Slammer, surgeon to the 97th . . . took snuff with everybody. . . .' Typical, like Dr. Slammer, of the period's respectable middle class, middle-aged professional men to whom

F

snuff was so important a thing, was Mr Perker, the 'little high-dried' lawyer who so constantly in the later pages of *Pickwick* 'took an argumentative pinch of snuff from an oblong silver box' in the intervals between ejaculations of 'really, my dear Sir, really'.

As a part of the make-up and stock in trade of the self-important Angelo Cyrus Bantam, whom the Pickwickians found discharging the duties of Master of Ceremonies at Bath, snuff was almost an essential; a successor to the office of Beau Nash would have been incomplete without a snuff-box. 'A charming young man of not much more than fifty, dressed in a very bright blue coat with resplendent buttons, black trousers, and the thinnest possible pair of highly-polished boots', was Mr. Bantam; he was a sparkling mass of jewellery and gold adornments; 'a gold snuff-box was lightly clasped in his left hand. . . . His snuff was prince's mixture'.

The personification of below-stairs dignity is John Smauker, Mr. Bantam's 'powdered-headed footman in gorgeous livery, and symmetrical stature', who introduced Sam Weller to the solemnly genteel society of Bath's gentlemen's gentlemen at the memorable soiree. In this refined circle snuff-taking of course has a place; what is proper to the master is proper to the man. Mr Smauker's accomplishment of snuffing without sneezing had been acquired by a system that should be remembered only in his own classic words:

> 'Do you do anything in this way, Sir?' inquired the tall footman, producing a small snuff-box with a fox's head on the top of it.
> 'Not without sneezing,' replied Sam.
> 'Why, it *is* difficult, Sir, I confess,' said the tall footman. 'It may be done by degrees, Sir. Coffee is the best practice. I carried coffee, Sir, for a long time. It looks very like rappee, Sir.'

Unlike the snuff-takers, most of the smokers appearing in *Pickwick Papers* are found to be young men following the fashion and acquiring the habit in spite of the discomforts of inexperience. Among the passengers outside the London and Bath coach,

> There was one young gentleman in an India-rubber cloak, who smoked cigars all day; and there was another young gentleman in a parody upon a great coat, who lighted a good many, and feeling obviously unsettled after the second whiff, threw them away when he thought nobody was looking at him.

Gradually and almost imperceptibly the numbers of snuff-takers grew fewer as smoking increased. Until 1820 the tobacco and cigars sold by Fribourg & Treyer represented no more than ten per cent of their business to ninety per cent snuff. By the first years of Queen Victoria's reign smoking materials were only slightly less in demand than snuff; in 1845 they were almost equally so; and by the late eighteen-fifties more smokers than snuffers were being supplied. At that time cigarettes had made themselves known and people were being tempted to smoke in a new way. First noted under the name of cigarettes in the Haymarket ledgers in 1852, they—or something like them—had been known in England for some ten years as paper-cigars. During and after the Crimean War the cigarette became increasingly popular; in the 'sixties it was accepted and in evidence all over Europe.

Import figures show decreasing quantities of the once fashionable foreign snuffs reaching this country throughout the Queen's reign, until eventually they became negligible. Snuffs ground and prepared in this country from imported tobaccos supplied the needs of the remaining snuff-takers, whose numbers had dwindled by the end of the nineteenth century to a minority overshadowed by so many smokers, though considerable enough to support an unobtrusive but flourishing British snuff industry.

The expansion of this industry from modest beginnings in the days of *carotte* grinding to its present scale of activity is, together with the consideration of some of the varieties of past and present-day snuffs, the concern of the following chapter. A word, however, is still owing to the modestly undemonstrative but by no means insignificant numbers of modern snuff-takers. It is a remarkable fact, and one which is well known to makers and vendors of snuff, that snuff-takers in Britain appear neither to have increased nor to have decreased very noticeably in numbers in recent years. Having once reached a certain level in the opening years of the present century, sales of snuff have varied but little; they continue in much the same course in spite of drastic increases in tobacco taxation of late. If there is a tendency in either direction, it is upward rather than downward; particularly since the last revenue attack on the tobacco consumer, which has raised the demand for snuff in some districts while reducing sales of smoking materials. The reason for this is not far to seek: snuff, while bearing taxation equally with tobacco in any other form, can seldom be consumed in quantities comparable to the tobacco or cigarettes used by an average smoker, and consequently recommends itself to many people as an economical alternative to smoking.

Since to affirm that snuff-taking maintains an important place among national habits is to contradict a widely-held belief that it is a dying fashion adhered to only by a few old-fashioned eccentrics, it is due to the statement to endorse it and attempt to substantiate its truth. The only reliable and relevant evidence is that provided by the snuff trade, and from several firms of manufacturers, blenders or specialist retailers who have been kind enough to contribute information a few typical opinions may be quoted. From one of the largest and best-known snuff mills in England comes the statement that snuff output

'Certainly has not decreased with us. We have no statistics but the trade is certainly much greater generally than fifty years ago'. The directors of a second famous mill in their more particular analysis of snuff consumption find that 'Consumption attained its peak between the two world wars. Heavy increases in the tobacco duty since 1914 have caused reduction but it seems to be on the increase again now. . . . Trade in recent years has increased very much more in southern England and is less in the north'. The last point is of interest in view of tradition having associated snuffing in the past with the north rather than the south. To Wales, according to the same authority, snuff is supplied in quantities which suggest that the snuffers there are at least as numerous as they are in England; to Scotland less is provided; in Ireland English snuff is in greater demand in Eire than in Ulster.

Both Northern Ireland and Eire, however, have several manufacturers to supply the greater part of a large and steadily maintained call for snuff, particularly for the distinctive Irish high-dried kind more fully dealt with in the next chapter. That the taste for this Irish snuff is shared by the people of Western Scotland is a fact noted by a member of the trade whose business it is in part to deal with the products of a major manufactory. Snuff-takers, he has noticed, are exactly what the supporters of so old a custom might be expected to be; namely a conservative and tradition-conscious community averse to any changes in their accustomed way of buying and using snuff. Local prejudices in favour of certain snuffs are very strong and innovations are generally regarded with disfavour. Changes in the packing and presentation of snuff are as unpopular and suspect as recommendations of unknown varieties. Long accustomed to buying their snuff 'loose' over the counter—taking it away in their own snuff-boxes or in little paper bags of a traditional triangular shape—from retailers who receive their supplies in bulk from the maker, snuff-takers in general ignore the existence of those neat little pocket tins or packets of snuff with which the trader has long sought to tempt them.

This reference of course is to established snuffers, the real devotees of the habit, and does not include the tyro and the smoker who uses snuff as an occasional alternative. The age at which people take to snuff and the regularity with which they maintain the demand for snuff are among other noteworthy facts observed by this authority:

> The interesting point about snuff is that sales do not seem to vary from year to year and although one does not often meet younger people who snuff, it is certain that new consumers must be starting every day, to take the place of those that die. My own opinion is—and this is not supported by any actual evidence, that snuff users do not usually take to the habit until about middle age.

Retailers, for the most part, support the evidence of manufacturers that snuff-taking shows no signs of dying out in Britain, although snuff is by no means equally popular in all districts. London, for instance, claims a distinct increase of late, while in East Anglia snuffers appear to grow fewer. Almost everywhere, however, in England, Scotland, Wales and Ireland snuff is sold in quantities which prove the omnipresence of the snuff-taker, who is to be met with in every walk of life, vocation and setting. Beyond the already noted observation that the majority of snuff-takers are in or past middle age, no qualifying limits can be applied to them: women who use snuff are perhaps fewer than men, and are less noticed since many of them indulge the habit with a discretion that almost amounts to secrecy, but are among the best customers at every snuff shop. The true, dyed-in-the-wool snuffer is seldom a smoker as well; practically never is he or she a cigarette-smoker. Often, though, heavy snuff-takers are found to be reformed smokers who have changed habits late in life.

Beyond these steady and substantial supporters of snuff are countless disciples of the smoke-when-you-can, snuff-when-you-can't school. As a rule they are the followers of callings which make smoking during working hours a difficulty or an impossibility. Such occupations are numerous and diverse; the carrying of a snuff-box is a long-established custom among tailors and cloth workers; in courts of law snuff has always had a place, and generations of barristers and judges have figured among the customers of the older snuff houses; drivers and conductors of many motor buses use snuff, as did their predecessors of the horse buses; snuff is taken in both Houses of Parliament, and in the Commons a communal snuff-box is maintained for the use of Members; as an antidote to coma snuff has certain advocates in the Civil Service; snuff-taking is traditional and very general among printers, compositors and night workers on newspapers, many hundreds of whom are regular patrons of the Fleet Street snuff shops.

It is no uncommon thing to hear a hardened snuff-taker say that he has bought snuff for thirty or forty years at the same shop, and that his liking for the habit developed from the acceptance of an occasional pinch while working as a young man in the snuffy atmosphere of a newspaper office or tailor's workroom. The last war produced many comparably snuffy places of toil, wherein the risk or offence of smoking was responsible for countless converts to the snuff-box. No inconsiderable number of these wartime converts today are counted as regular patrons by snuff-sellers; doctors, with soldiers and sailors of senior rank and members of every profession, are among them. At least one doctor has blended M. & B. with snuff for his personal use, without, it is believed, sharing the ingenious prescription with his patients.

CHAPTER IV

The Varieties and Preparation of Snuff

DURING the seventeenth century and for long into the eighteenth such snuff as was prepared in Britain was ground by hand. Large rasps which were not unlike heavy nutmeg-graters were used by early snuff-sellers—among them the apothecaries and quacks who did so much to promote snuff-taking by recommending it as a cure or palliative—to reduce to powder tobacco made up and imported in *carotte* form. Rolls or twists of compressed tobacco, *carottes* were supplied in a shape roughly resembling a carrot; in size they were large enough to produce, when ground, from three to four pounds of snuff. *Carottes*, too, were bought by snuff-takers who preferred to grind their own powder, using for the purpose smaller rasps; many of them of pocket size and incorporated in snuff-boxes which were divided to hold a piece of *carotte* and the snuff produced from it. Pestles and mortars also were used at an early date to reduce leaf tobacco to snuff consistency; the tobacco was dried to brittleness, powdered in a mortar, and finally sieved through a widely-woven cloth.

The first mills used to grind snuff were turned by hand, like coffee-mills. As far back as in the sixteenth century Brazilian Indians were using mills of this kind which in all probability were unheard of in England before the days of general snuff-taking in the eighteenth century. The snuff-makers of Brazil were in fact the pioneers of the industry, practised and experienced in tobacco-grinding long before any European nation used snuff. Brazilian methods and skill inspired the later snuff experts

VII Chased and Enamelled Gold Snuff-box (Swiss, c. 1820)

Of pocket size and incorporating a musical box. The scene on the hinged lid is painted on the *underside* of glass and mounted over a chiselled gold surface to produce the sunray effect

VIII Silver Snuff-boxes

Divided box with three compartments and rasp (*left*). George III box shaped to the pocket (*right*)

of Europe as one by one the countries adopted the snuff habit and snuff-making became a lucrative business.

Though England was many years behind most of her neighbours in following the snuffing fashion, when at last she did so there were, as we have seen, no half measures about the craze for it which swept the country. Spreading so rapidly, the habit overtook England before the country could boast snuff-makers sufficiently numerous or skilled to compete with business on a large scale. The possibilities opened up by the all too sudden demand for snuff were, it seems, quickly realised, but the immediate benefits were reaped by importing rather than making snuff. While snuff-making progressed slowly as Englishmen gradually acquired knowledge of the art from abroad, and refinements were introduced by such men as Lillie coming from older snuff-taking countries, something very much like a gold mine developed for merchants and others able to secure supplies of foreign snuffs. These finished products of countries already adept in the crafts of maturing, fermenting, blending and grinding tobaccos to various grains—in some cases also in growing the leaf—and equally cunning in the final touches of flavouring, captured the English market. Reaching this country ready for use, tightly packed in wooden casks, kegs or—in the case of some of the finer blends—sealed in leaden canisters or glass bottles, foreign snuffs in enormous variety filled the snuff-boxes of the majority of fashionable snuff-takers. Prepared snuffs, too, were imported in cake or *carotte* form, needing only the application of a rasp to reduce them to grain. In one form or the other foreign snuffs held until the end of the period of fashionable snuffing the place they took at its beginning as socially the most favoured snuffs, heavily outnumbering in their varieties the home-prepared snuffs of England, Scotland and Ireland.

Foreign snuffs were well known to seventeenth century

snuffers in Britain and in small quantities were imported by London traders. The responsibility for the first bulk importation on a large scale rests, however, with Sir George Rooke and his seamen, who introduced their huge captured consignment of Havana snuff in 1702. From its place of seizure this cargo became known in England as Vigo Snuff: its work in propagating the snuffing habit was soon done, and the shipment, great though it was, was not long in being absorbed. Thereafter followed direct importations of Havana snuffs, prepared from Cuban tobacco and sold under such names as Cabinet Havannah. With them came snuffs from Brazil, so long and more than any other country associated with snuff production, and others from Virginia, Martinique and Buenos Ayres. Many more prepared snuffs from South America and the West Indies were to become popular in Britain and were to be imported steadily in large quantities by the end of Queen Anne's reign.

To the snuffs supplied direct from the West were added countless kinds ground—sometimes from native tobacco —in European countries where snuff was used, and its preparation studied, before it was widely adopted in England. French, German, Italian, Spanish and Dutch snuffs in manifold forms all had their advocates in eighteenth century Britain. The French kinds were perhaps the most numerous and the most frequently remembered in contemporary chronicles; among them were dark coloured snuffs ground from home-grown leaf and others produced from American tobaccos, and in some of them the flower perfumes of Provence were used to impart flavour. Germany, too, grew tobacco used in certain snuff blends. Italian snuffs were specifically mentioned in the advertisements of the earlier English vendors, though they were less in demand than those from Spain. Seville in fact emerged as the headquarters of the snuff industry in Europe, its people following the Brazilians in making themselves famous for their blends; the quantities produced in this City of Snuff were enormous, the varieties several, and elsewhere in Europe the name of Seville used as prefix to a snuff was generally held to imply superiority.

Snuff records of the eighteenth and early nineteenth century bristle with the names of foreign snuffs sold and used in Britain, many of them clearly denoting their places of origin. Half the nations of the world are represented among these names; even India is associated with snuffing by the royally favoured Masulipatam. There is a pleasantly romantic sound about many of these titles under which snuff was sold, and even—if it is permissible to use the word in such a connection—an aromatic implication seeming to hint at distinctions of *bouquet* and pungency, and at secrets of blending and flavouring which, always jealously guarded, in too many instances have been completely unrecorded and forgotten. No complete catalogue of the varieties of imported snuffs survives, but the following list, compiled from trade records and contemporary literature, includes most of those which were particularly distinguished and popular in Britain throughout the eighteenth century and the earlier years of the nineteenth. Imperfect as it is, it serves to suggest the magnitude of the scale of snuff importation and to recall the principal foreign sources of supply:

Abbeville	Cuba	Gros Grain
Amsterdam	Curaçoa	Havre
Arras	Dieppe	Light Dutch
Bergamotte	Domingo	Lisbon
Bolongaro	Dunkirk	Longueville
Bordeaux	Dutch Bran	Macouba
Brazil	Dutch Carotte	Mannheim
Brussels	Étrennes	Marina
Buenos Ayres	Façon de Paris	Marino de Leipsic
Bureau	Frankfort	Martinique
Cabinet Havannah	French Carotte	Masulipatam
Cologne	French Prize	Milan

Mississippi	Port au Prince	Spanish Bran
Montagne	Ransio	Spanish Sabilla
Montoban	Robillard	Strasbourg
Morlaix	Rapé de Lyons	Tongear
Morocco	Rouen	Vigo
Moyquer	St. Vincent	Villefranche
Old Paris	Scholten	Violet Strasbourg
Oronoko	Seville	Virginia Carotte
Paris		

Only the bare descriptions under which these snuffs were sold are given in the list; most, it should be remembered, were available in more than one size of grain and were then distinguished by the further descriptions of Coarse, Medium or Fine, or more often the French equivalents, *Gros*, *Demi-gros* and *Fin*. French terms were widely adopted or adapted by British snuff traders, the more punctilious of whom were wont to label their jars holding snuff of French origin with the prefix *Tabac de*; *raper* or *rapé* became Rappee when used to name an English snuff; *carotte* in time lost its original meaning and became a usual name for ready-ground snuffs of more than one kind. The *Gros Grain* mentioned in the list was, incidentally, the name of a once popular and distinguished snuff not to be confused with the general term applied to varied snuffs of coarse grinding; *Bergamotte*, too, in the eighteenth century meant more than the flavour it suggests and designated a select blend.

Among these imported kinds were to be found the perfection of fine snuff-making, the products of thoughtful selection in the first choice of suitable tobaccos, of practised artistry in milling, blending or flavouring and of time in giving maturity. The previous chapters have introduced many of them as the choices of the critical connoisseurs of the past. Writing of some of these refined preparations of the eighteenth and early nineteenth centuries in his book on *The Old Snuff House*, George Evans has referred to them as something to which no modern comparisons exist. In most cases the flavour and fragrance were the result of skill in blending diverse suitable and matured tobaccos, a natural flavour rather than one imparted artificially with perfumes and scent extracts. Much blending of different kinds of imported snuffs was carried out by English firms in former times; mention in the previous chapter of the 'sorts' especially blended for customers and the extracts from Fribourg & Treyer's recipe book will have given an idea of the lengths to which this practice was carried. Some of these fine snuffs, in the opinion of the same authority, could be reproduced under modern conditions, while others it would be quite impossible to make.

Mr. Evans's authoritative notes on some of the snuffs particularly associated with his firm in the past should be remembered. Martinique he describes as a snuff light in colour and character and possessed of a distinctive flavour which owed nothing to applied scent or essence; Martinique from George IV's collection was in great demand in the years immediately following the King's death, when it was sold under the name of King's Martinique and commanded a price of one guinea a pound, almost double the cost of lesser snuffs. Masulipatam was exceedingly strong in flavour; rather too much for a delicate nose when used alone, it was much employed for blending with milder snuffs. Macouba, too, added distinction to many blends, its powerful fragrance being an imparted one derived from Otto of Roses. Both Masulipatam and Macouba were sold in bottles, not unlike pint claret bottles with narrow necks, from which the snuff was extracted with the aid of a long spoon or skewer. Snuff of Macouba character, differing from that of the old days in its basic tobacco but similarly scented with Otto of Roses, is still on the market; so, too, is an Old Paris snuff which is prepared from an especially ground base with the aid of an old private recipe. One of the most peculiar as well as popular of the listed snuffs was Spanish Bran[1]; its popularity was established in Britain by mid-eighteenth century and lasted for more than eighty years, while its peculiarity lay in the fact that it was sold accompanied by a small flask of a Spanish scented vinegar called *Vinagrillo*, which was used at frequent intervals to restore loss of flavour and moisture. Unique in another respect was Spanish Sabilla, since it was sold more often to people who used it for cleaning their teeth than to those who took it as snuff. Sabilla was very finely ground and almost red in colour. In this connection it should be noted, perhaps, that snuffs varied, and still do vary, as much in colour as in grain; drapers may use the term 'snuff-colour' to describe certain light brown materials, but snuff in fact may be any shade of brown, or nearly white, black or a russet red.

Earlier records provide a key to the making and blending of one or two more of the distinguished snuffs given in the list above, and give a hint of the elaborate, prolonged and painstaking processes followed. That famous French snuff, *Gros Grain,* for instance, was ground in the first place from James River and Amersfoort tobaccos in equal proportions. In its final stages it was given a highly spiced flavour by treating it with a composite liquid known as a 'sauce', made up of fine French brandy, burgundy, salt, soda, cream of tartar, a sweet syrup, and tamarinds, together with several minor ingredients. Another of the highly scented snuffs was Morocco; the fragrance in this case was imparted not by a liquid essence but by blending finely ground rose petals with snuff made from the midribs or stalks of Virginia tobacco, added to twice as great a quantity of snuff made from St. Omar tobacco. After sifting, the blend was damped down with salt and water; lastly

---

[1] Spanish Bran was the highest priced snuff noted as having been in George IV's collection; it was sold at £3 per pound.

cream and salts of tartar were used in perfecting the mixture before packing in leaden canisters.

Contained in some of the old receipts for the flavouring and finishing of once popular snuffs is a suggestion of an interest as great and a care as studied as those lavished on the distilling of subtle monastic liqueurs. The comparison is one which might even be carried as far as tracing herbal and floral flavouring agents which were used as commonly in the one industry as in the other. Snuff-takers themselves often showed a good deal of ingenuity and enterprise in devising elaborate snuff recipes to add to the formulæ of professional blenders and snuff houses; the mere blending of several established varieties of imported snuff ranked as child's-play compared with the discoveries made by some of the more inspired amateur seekers of the perfect fragrance. One such private recipe must be quoted as an example; it is transcribed from the original manuscript note, in which it appears in a not over-legible hand and in faded ink but without key to its author or date:

To 10 lbs. of Snuff (which it is indispensable should be of a sweet Brazil character) take first 1½ lbs. of the best French Plums. Let them simmer for at least 5 hours until reduced to the feel of a soft . . . pulp, adding while simmering about 2 ozs. of grated Chapzugar Cheese; add thereto while simmering 1½ Salt—When the plums are sufficiently soft rub them through a cane sieve in order to separate the stones—then spread out your snuff and force the plums through a wire sieve on to the snuff—mix it well up with your hands and 1½ pints of best Olive or Almond Oil and work the whole twice through the wire sieve: add about two glasses of Port wine lees.

If you can get any Jaggaree dissolve 1½ lbs. in hot water with 2 ozs. Chapzugar and salt, if necessary a little wine lees—This is a much better recipe and requires no Plums—but the foundation *must* be a *sweet luscious flavour'd* snuff.

Unlike the fashionable foreign snuffs of eighteenth century association, the contemporary varieties of British ground snuffs were not numerous. British Rappee was the principal product of English makers who during this period emerged as the founders of a later flourishing industry. Setting aside the various famous mixtures which were sold by the snuff-houses, as having been mainly, if not entirely, composed of foreign snuffs, history and trade records produce little reference to English-ground snuff beyond rappee. Rappee, however, was a very elastic term, covering as it did Black Rappee, Brown Rappee and improved varieties sold under such names as Imperial Rappee. Basically plain snuffs, rappees also were sold with diverse added scented flavours; originally, too, they were coarse in grain as the French derivation of their name suggests, but later were made in medium and fine grain. Like the majority of the imported snuffs, rappees were sold in a slightly damp condition and were known as moist snuffs. Scotch, Welsh and Irish snuffs, on the other hand, were dry in character, and for the most part were light both in grain and colour. The traditional Scotch snuff of the past was a finely milled powder often owing its lightness of colour to the midribs or central stalks of the tobacco leaf; today the term Scotch snuff is commonly used in the trade to describe the lighter, finer ground types of English-made snuff. Welsh snuffs were similarly fine powders, sometimes high-dried or toasted in the manner of the Irish. Of the character and distinction of Irish high-dried snuffs, ground from midribs and of 'toasted' flavour, much remains to be said, both of their past associations and their present popularity.

Too often authors and note-makers of other days have left us with casual references to presumably well-known contemporary snuffs without a hint of their character or quality. Not a few of such passing mentions clearly indicate Scotch and Irish varieties that were esteemed either widely or locally for some particular virtue or distinguishing flavour the nature of which has gone, and must remain, unrecorded. About Gillespie snuff we know now as little as of the merits of that 'little Provision of the best Preston Pans snuff' which is remembered, together with a 'bottle of Highland Snishon', in Hull's *Letters* of 1761. The Coarse Irish figuring in old trade records makes it clear that the finely ground snuffs generally associated with Ireland were by no means the only ones, and it is a reasonable conclusion that there was nothing fine about the hand-ground *smutchin* of seventeenth century Ireland, though we are left to guess at the distinctions of such formerly popular Irish snuffs as Lambkin's Brand. Happily, however, less obscurity clouds the history of High Toast, long established and still accepted as the traditional Irish snuff.

Sheer chance provided snuff-takers with a fresh and distinctive flavour which owed nothing to perfume when Lundy Foot, a Dublin snuff-maker, discovered how palatable a thing was toasted snuff; thereby bringing fame and profit to himself and the most popular of Irish snuffs to the market. The most reliable of several versions of the old story has it that early in the eighteenth century Lundy Foot was established in a modest way of business as a maker and purveyor of highly dried snuff. The preparation of the light, dust-like powder of high dried snuff was, and is, a prolonged business, demanding that the tobacco stalks from which the snuff is ground should first be dried in a nicely regulated heat. It was while drying stalks with a view to grinding later a large quantity of snuff that Lundy Foot turned an accident to good account. His practice it was to kiln-dry his tobacco stalks overnight, leaving them, while he went home to bed, in charge of one Larry, his assistant. It was Larry's duty to watch and regulate the heat, seeing to it that the drying process reached only that point which his master considered perfection. Reliable enough when sober, Larry yet had a weakness: poteen proved too much for him on a night when an unusually large batch of tobacco was

G

under treatment. His master found him the next morning,
lying unconscious beside the kiln; the neglected stalks
had been over-dried to the point of charring, and apparently ruined. Loth to face their complete loss, Lundy
Foot ground some in the hope that they might yet
provide snuff good enough to sell at a cheap rate to the
undiscriminating. On trying a few pinches, he found to
his amazement that the slightly burnt or toasted flavour
was pleasant and entirely original. Before long the Lundy
Foot High Toast speciality was the rage of Dublin; later
it was to make his name familiar far beyond his native city.

High Toast, prepared today by a number of Irish firms,
and the Rappees, ground by as many English mills,
are among the snuff names which link the past with the
present. They survive from the days of hand-grinding of
comparatively small quantities of tobacco into a time
when home-manufactured snuff is produced on a scale
not generally guessed at, nor indeed likely to be believed
by those who suppose snuff-taking to be a dead or rapidly
dying custom. The processes of snuff-making during this
long period have undergone many changes, which, if
treated chronologically and conscientiously, would
amount to a long and extremely tedious trade history;
recent methods, however, may be described as briefly as
possible and compared occasionally with those of the past.

The first stage of snuff production in this country may
be allowed to be the importation of suitable tobaccos.
Formerly these chosen leafs were chiefly of American
origin: of later years, as Empire tobaccos have improved
in quality and dollar considerations have had to be faced,
an increasing proportion of Dominion growths have been
used by snuff-makers, as by manufacturers of cigarettes
and smoking tobaccos. Beyond the selection of appropriate tobaccos lies the choice of different parts of the
plant to provide the basic characters of varying snuffs:
stalks or midribs are used in making Irish high dried

snuffs, some of those usually referred to as Scotch and Welsh and most that belong to the drier and lighter coloured types; the soft parts of the leaf may go to the making of the moister and darker snuffs; and in many kinds leaves, stalks and what are called 'smalls' together provide a basis.

An authority of nearly a century ago described among the preliminaries of snuff-making the cutting of the leaf (either midrib or soft parts) into small pieces, which then were damped down with water before being packed in bins, where they remained for a period lasting from two months to as long as two years. The essentials of this process are still followed: when it has been cut into lengths, the tobacco is damped—sometimes with a salt solution, the mildness of which is dictated by one of the several laws governing the preparation of snuff and smoking tobacco—and piled into large vats, where it is allowed a long period of fermentation. While undergoing this 'cure', as it is called, the fermenting tobacco is turned from time to time, and the temperature is regulated by the frequent use of long-handled thermometers, it not being allowed to rise above approximately 130 degrees, Fahrenheit. Evaporation during this process cleanses the tobacco by depriving it of natural properties which would prove unpalatable and possibly harmful if allowed to remain in snuff.

Irish High Toast and other high dried snuffs demand variations in their treatment, in that the stalks or midribs, after damping with either water or an alkaline liquid and fermenting, are dried or 'toasted' to the required pitch in what various authorities have described as ovens, kilns and furnaces, but which the large scale makers of High Toast in the present day refer to as drying rooms.

In the matter of grinding his snuff the manufacturer has made many concessions to progress. After rasps, graters, pestles and mortars and hand-turned mills were left

behind, he took a lead from the flour-miller in making
use of water-mills and windmills. It is possible that wind
power was used to grind snuff in Britain, as it certainly
was in Holland; at least one water-mill deriving its
power from a stream is still to be seen in England at
Sharrow Mills in Sheffield, where it was grinding the
whole of a very large output of snuff until steam power
was installed some sixty years ago. Machine-driven mills
on an elaborate scale are used now in all large snuff
factories, grinding tobacco to the finest possible powder
or to coarse or medium grain as the type of snuff—from
light Scotch to coarse Rappee—may require. To cite as
an example Westbrook Mill, another of Sheffield's large
scale sources of snuff: one may see there a succession of
mills, each grinding a certain kind of snuff, and each
working isolated and enclosed in a cupboard-like com-
partment so that the fine dust which pervades all snuff-
grinders' premises may be kept within reasonable bounds.
Passage through riddles of varying gauge and—in the
case of the finest snuffs—repeated grinding ensures the
production of the exact grain needed.

Moisture content is another important consideration
in the ritual of snuff-making. Tobacco, quickly and easily
absorbing moisture as it does, is sent to this country in
as dry a state as possible, treatment having reduced its
retained moisture to less than fifteen per cent so that the
exorbitant rate of duty charged on imported leaf (increased from 3s. 8d. a pound before 1914, to £2 18s. 2d.
at the present time) may be payable on as little water as
is feasible. Moisture therefore must be added to most
English snuffs to produce that pleasant smoothness
belonging to them when they are sent out from the mills,
closely packed in the large tins which have replaced the
kegs, canisters or earthen jars of the past.

The processes outlined up to this point are those of
wholesale snuff manufacturers, who in modern times are

represented by the various specialist firms, several of
which are of very old foundation and all of which are
concerned solely with the production of snuff, and by a
number of tobacco manufacturers who combine snuff-
making with the production of cigarettes and pipe
tobaccos. Both manufacturers and the few remaining
retail snuff-houses that sell their own flavoured blends,
however, carry the preparation of snuff far beyond this
point. Plain, unscented snuffs are supplied to those
snuff-takers who prefer them; for the rest there are
infinite varieties of snuffs with subtle fragrances and
flavours imparted by scenting and blending.

A good deal of mystery has been and always will be
associated with the final phases of flavouring and scenting
snuff, since the proportions in which flavouring agents
are used and the means by which they are applied in
many cases are contained in private formulæ which, very
naturally, are kept dark by their holders. It is possible
and permissible, though, to indicate the lines followed,
without disclosing any of those trade secrets usually
coupled with such phrases as 'closely kept' or 'jealously
guarded'. Briefly, a snuff in itself unflavoured and usually
called a base—or a blend of two or three such plain snuffs
of the required size of grain—is treated with certain
essential oils or essences in carefully measured proportions to make a scented snuff. The main flavouring ingredients of many of the more popular scented snuffs
are obvious and are indicated by the names under which
such snuffs are sold; Peppermint, Wallflower and Car-
nation snuffs are examples. These and many others with
titles less indicative of the perfumes they contain are in
no way the prerogative of one blender or manufacturer
but commonly are made by several firms, different brands
of given snuffs varying slightly according to the proportions and qualities of the ingredients. Other scented
blends there are which remain the speciality or unique

preparation of a certain factory or snuff-shop holding a
formula as unknown to other members of the trade as
to the outside world.

By no means all the flavouring ingredients given in
old snuff recipes would be permitted under later laws in
this country: others certainly would prove extravagantly
costly under modern conditions. The tobacco duty at its
present rate would reduce to absurdity some of the
lavishly wasteful treatments advocated by authorities of
the time and type of Monsieur Lillie, who thought
nothing of sluicing away pounds of good snuff in successive soakings, strainings, dryings and re-soakings in
dilute perfumes. Of the Tobacco Acts, which limit to
harmless ingredients the preparations used in all the
stages of snuff- and tobacco-making, little need be said
here, except that they ensure the purity of modern snuff,
are unbelievably dull reading in themselves, and date
back to days when dangerous but economical substances
of many kinds were to be found in snuff 'blends'.

Among the harmless and allowable flavourings used in
snuff-scenting are essential oils of flowers like the violet
and wallflower, spices like cloves and cinnamon, and
extracts made from lavender and peppermint, bergamot,
bitter almonds and certain fragrant barks and beans.
There is no mystery about these and many other essential
oils and spirit solutions being employed; any trade
secrets there may be are those of proportions, methods
of application, blending and manipulation. Some snuffs
derive their fragrance from a single flower essence; others
from composite scents. Here and there a modern scented
snuff has as its predominating aroma an attar noted as
having been used in one of the distinguished imported
snuffs of the past, as in the cases of Otto of Roses; there
are many rose-scented snuffs today, in the perfecting of
one of the more exotic of which the blenders are still
using a flask of attar bought over a century ago.

More often, perhaps, than any other single source of
relish, have Tonquin beans been used with snuff, both
by blenders and by snuff-takers themselves. The flavour
of snuffs formerly sold under such names as Tonquine
and Tonka was provided by powdered or liquid preparations from these beans. In whole form Tonquin beans are
still stocked by the older snuff-shops, and are sold in
fair quantities to customers who follow the time honoured custom of carrying a single bean in a snuff-box,
or keeping two or three of them in a jar of snuff. Used
in this way, the beans impart to snuff a little of their
aromatic content, a peculiar pungency increasing the
snuff's titillating powers, giving it piquancy and having
a tonic influence on snuff that has been allowed to grow
savourless. So old is the association of Tonquin and snuff
that it well may trace back to the time when snuff-production centred in Brazil: Tonquin beans are natives of
that country and of British Guiana, where they and the
forest trees that grow them are called Rumara. Yet
another name is given to the Tonquin when it is reduced
to the scent essence known to perfumers as Cumarin.

Other than the carriers of Tonquin beans in their snuff-
boxes there are not many survivors among present day
snuff-takers of the amateur dabblers in snuff-scenting who
once were so numerous, and who devoted so much time
and serious thought to seeking elusive flavours. Still
occasionally to be met with, however, are those who mix
for their own use two or more of the popular kinds of
snuff. Familiar, too, to most snuff-takers is the man who
delights in making a mystery of the contents of his box;
who, while freely offering pinches to anyone who cares to
sample his mixture, and accepting encomiums with
obvious pleasure, will pass off any enquiries as to his
snuff's origin with some such evasive answer as 'A
private blend of my own', or 'Something specially made
up for me in London'—or Norwich, or Bristol, or any

town likely to contain a specialist snuff-house where blending is still practised.

Almost every tobacconist today is a seller of prepared snuff, stocking one or two of the more popular kinds, but the specialising snuffman who may be also a blender has become a rarity. It is in our older cities that the latter is to be found most often, sometimes carrying on in appropriately ancient premises a business founded or flourishing in the days of lavish and general snuff-taking. Occasionally such snuff-shops are distinguished by a Highland figure or some other traditional sign of the trade, and within will be found to cherish old associations to the extent of exhibiting bygone blending implements, snuff-jars and casks which, together with certain relevant prints and a collection of snuff-boxes, may make up quite a little museum of snuff relics. All too few, these are pleasant and fitting places for the continuance of a trade too old and distinguished to consort happily with such things as chromium-plated counters and petrol-lighters.

With the manufacture and wholesale distribution of snuff two English towns long have been and still remain closely and particularly associated. Sheffield is one and Kendal the other of the two principal English sources of snuff supply at the present time. Mills in both places are owned or directed by descendants of snuff-makers who were at work within the eighteenth century, when were laid the modest foundations of British snuff-production. The two Sheffield producers already mentioned both trace their origin to the industry of Joseph Wilson, who was making snuff two hundred years ago and whose descendants continue to make snuff in each of the mills. At least one of three well-known Kendal mills claims an eighteenth-century foundation. Elsewhere in England, as in Ireland, the business of snuff-making flourishes in widely scattered and sometimes unexpected places, and more often than not it is practised by long-established

Houses. To particularise these snuff sources would entail compiling a small directory which would contain, among others, the names of firms in Liverpool and Devizes, in Birmingham and Bristol, both snuff-makers pure-and-simple and general manufacturers of tobacco products: Northern Ireland would be represented by several Houses in Belfast, and Eire by those of Dundalk and other places farther south.

Chambers's *Encyclopædia* of 1727 stated that 'the kinds of snuff and their several names are infinite'. The statement was made when the snuffing fashion was at its height and countless varieties and blends of foreign snuffs were on the market, but it might fairly be applied to the home-produced snuffs of today if all the products—both scented and plain—of the various snuff-traders were counted under the different names applied to them. Additions are ever being made to a long list of proprietary prepared brands and blends. Distinct types of snuff, on the other hand, remain limited to those bearing such widely known names as S.P., Kendal Brown and High Toast. These are general descriptions of snuff types rather than names; they indicate kinds which are ground by a number of manufacturers and are not the prerogative of particular firms. The three mentioned are among the oldest, as they are certainly the most in demand, of the snuffs of Britain and Ireland.

Probably S.P. is the best-known kind of snuff made and sold in England; particularly in Southern England and in London it is used in enormous quantities, being sold by innumerable tobacconists and small traders and bought by thousands of snuff-takers to many of whom it is the one and only snuff. By the majority S.P. is preferred plain, though sold also with scented flavours for those who like them: plain S.P. has a natural tobacco flavour. In character a Scotch-type snuff, it is finely ground, smooth, and light brown in colour. Whence or how it derived its name is a riddle to which only the forgotten snuff-makers of the past knew the answer; of many explanations and suggestions that have been made the most probable and one of the most recent is that it dates from days when the abbreviation Sp: was used by snuffmen to denote imported Spanish snuffs, to some of which S.P. perhaps bears a resemblance.

Kendal Brown proclaims in its name its place of origin and principal source. The name is one known over most of the world as that of an old and typical English snuff of a medium coarse grain, richly brown in colour. Both plain and scented Kendal Brown snuffs are on the market. They are popular with snuff-takers who prefer a large to a fine grain throughout England, especially in the northern counties. In Eastern Scotland, too, the popular taste has long been for the scented varieties of Kendal Brown and that which is flavoured with peppermint.

Snuff tastes divide Scotland in that the people of the West favour the light, dry, almost white, finely-ground High Toast of Ireland, rather than heavy-grained snuff. Here, though, as in the East, there is a marked liking for peppermint and similarly strong flavours. Local tradition dictates that these flavourings should be administered by the retailer, and snuff pre-flavoured by the manufacturer is generally eschewed; 'Irish with a dash of Peppermint' is an order commonly to be heard at the shops of snuff-sellers and tobacconists in that part of Scotland which is nearest to Ireland.

In Ulster and throughout most of snuff-taking Ireland High Toast snuffs are the choice of the majority. Generally they are used with their essential and distinctive toasted flavour unrelieved by other relishes. In England comparatively few people have acquired a taste for snuff of this kind, and nothing perhaps could better illustrate how local and conservative are snuff preferences than the way in which High Toast is shovelled out almost by the hundredweight in the shops of its native country, and in that part of Scotland where Irish influences are noticeable, while in London it would be hard to find more than two or three dealers who sell it.

Among other old types of snuff which survive are British Rappees, still to be found both black and brown in colour and of medium and light grain; plain Rappees are less popular with snuff-takers than they were, but are used by blenders in the making of some favourite scented snuffs. The ancient name of French Carotte, too, still figures in the list of distinguished snuffs as the product of a Bristol firm dating from the eighteenth century.

British snuff for many years has supplied the home market. Added to this must be remembered a considerable trade in snuffs made in Britain for export. The tastes of many nations abroad are catered for, and among them are to be counted some of the countries which formerly flooded the English market with snuffs of their own production. It is a noteworthy fact, though one outside the set limits of these pages, that snuff-takers form a part of the population of every country. Tastes in, and ideas about snuff, however, vary enormously; and the word snuff has more meanings than the use of it in Britain would suggest. In the United States of America, for instance, where snuff-making is a formidable industry, snuff is of two distinct species: snuffs for sniffing, both American and some imported from England, and snuffs for chewing, which are absorbed by the tongue rather than the nose and generally are known as Copenhagen snuffs. South Africa and India are customers for British snuff, while in both countries native snuffs are yet made by hand from dried and salted tobacco. European snuffs, too, still have many forms and flavours, among them those of the home-grown tobaccos of France and Germany.

CHAPTER V

Snuff-boxes

FEW objects of personal use or adornment have been fashioned in a greater number of forms than have snuff-boxes, and not many such objects, watches not excepted, have inspired more artistry and skilled craftsmanship in their designing and embellishing. Snuff-boxes have been made at every period from the seventeenth century to the present day and, if the term in its widest meaning is allowed to include such allied containers as the snuff-bottles of China and the horn snuff-mulls of Scotland, have been produced in almost every country in the world. In the hey-day of snuff-taking snuff-boxes earned themselves remembrance in the histories of several European nations as the constant companions or playthings of eminent men and women, the rewards of merit and virtue, the bribes of treachery and intrigue, even as the means of attempted murder or escape from death. In times more recent the beauty and value of fine snuff-boxes, those fashioned from gold and precious materials or decorated with the work of major artists, have ensured them places in the literature of art. At all times since snuffing first became a fashion in Europe the snuff-box has recommended itself to the connoisseur and collector of small objects of beautiful workmanship, and is to be found represented in every important private or public collection of such things. It might also be said of snuff-boxes that they have been made of every possible, workable material to which a name can be given: mineral, animal and vegetable products, together with many manufactured compositions.

Snuff-boxes of all origins, ages, and materials in the aggregate represent a theme so formidable as to appear to be inexhaustible. Confined, however, within the same modest limits that have been allowed to snuff in the foregoing pages, the subject is reduced to one embracing only the principal and noteworthy types of boxes used by British snuff-takers in the past. With boxes of British origin are included those made abroad but widely adopted in Britain and still well represented by examples in the hands of collectors, museums and antique dealers in this country; and occasionally, too, a Continental box, as much as an English or a Scottish one, must be permitted to retain an anecdote having a place in its history or associations.

Gold, more than any other of the many substances from which snuff-boxes have been made, must always be associated with fine and beautiful workmanship. Throughout the eighteenth century and for a considerable part of the nineteenth noted goldsmiths in at least half a dozen European countries were devoting much of their time and talents to the designing and production of the snuff-box, acknowledging it to be what it then was—an essential part of the personal equipment of the distinguished. Snuff-box making was a recognised and highly profitable branch of the jeweller's art in which every possible form of applied decoration that ingenuity could suggest was employed to embellish and elaborate boxes fashioned from gold.

The more usual means of decorating gold boxes were those of engraving or incising designs in the surface; of chasing the metal by tapping or pressing it from the outside; and of producing *repoussé* or raised patterns by beating the material in an outward direction from the back. Pictorial decoration of every kind from the classical scene to the personal portrait can be found on gold snuffboxes; in enamel fired upon the gold; in painting on panels of porcelain, ivory and the under surface of glass, and on other materials set in lids, sides and bases; and in cameos or the embossed or carved medallions of such substances as tortoise-shell and mother-of-pearl. Diamonds and precious stones of all colours were set in the lids of many boxes to form monograms or more ambitious designs, and a single gem of size and worth frequently acted as the point of thumb pressure to open hinged boxes. Golds of different colours—obtained by varying mixtures of alloy—were sometimes assembled to form contrasts on a single box. In some very elaborate specimens are to be seen combinations of several of the forms of decoration mentioned, together with others rarer and more complicated.

The most numerous and certainly the most lavishly decorated of fine gold snuff-boxes are those which came from France. Over a period dating at least from the reign of Louis XIII to the outbreak of the French Revolution and continued in the time of Napoleon I, named and noted Parisian specialists were producing superb minor works of art in the form of snuff-boxes so perfectly contrived and finished as to be sought by connoisseurs of the beautiful in many countries, and paid for in some cases at the rate of several thousand livres for a single box. Many of the French boxes of this period came to Britain, where some remain in private collections and museums. Magnificent, too, if as a rule less ornately decorated, are surviving English gold boxes bearing London hall-marks of the reigns of the four Georges. These are often characterised by an appearance of workmanlike solidity as though the boxes were meant for hard service in a man's pocket as well as for ornament, in contrast to the feminine and somewhat toy-like suggestion in much of the French workmanship. Engraving and carving on a simple gold surface appears more usually on English boxes than the enamel or painted scenes beloved of the Paris craftsmen and much inspired by the work of such contemporary painters as Boucher and Fragonard. Other sources of fine workmanship in gold snuff-boxes which found their way to England were Sweden, Germany, Switzerland and Austria. Oblong, square, oval and round were usual shapes in the boxes of all countries; in size they generally allowed for the carrying of from a quarter to a half ounce of snuff in such boxes as were intended for the pocket. By far the greater part of gold snuff-boxes must be counted pocket boxes, in general distinguished by a hinged lid, but in this material as in others table boxes were made of larger size and often with a detachable, separate top.

Pocket as well as table boxes sometimes incorporated additions or devices unrelated to snuff which added considerably to their weight and bulk. False bottoms or double lids concealed secret small compartments; miniature portraits that remained hidden until a catch was pressed or a panel opened; inset watches; or tiny and delicately made musical boxes capable of playing two or three airs when wound up with a little key in the manner of a watch. There were no limits to the ingenuity of those who contrived novel and elaborate boxes for snuff, as well as similar small containers or caskets intended for comfits, patches or trinkets, which often are loosely described as snuff-boxes.

The collecting of fine snuff-boxes as objects of art and beauty is no modern hobby. Though the making of such collections since the vogue for fashionable snuff-taking died out has been carried to lengths which qualify it for a place among the popular pastimes of millionaires of recent times, and snuff-box collections on dispersal occasionally sell for such high figures as to make them front page news, comparable collectors were as active and enthusiastic when snuffing was general and the most gifted of the designers of snuff-boxes were at work. In the eighteenth century were connoisseurs of the calibre of Prince Louis Ferdinand of Bourbon Conti, who had collected before the year 1776 no fewer than eight hundred specimens of snuff-box art. Ten years later than that date occurred the death of Frederick the Great of Prussia with whom the amassing of snuff-boxes was a passion, in spite of the fact that he seldom carried a box, preferring to have a pocket filled with a loose supply of the snuff which he consumed in such enormous quantities.

Napoleon Bonaparte could be counted almost the equal of Frederick of Prussia both as a taker of snuff and a devotee of the finer types of box made to contain it. Napoleon's use of snuff is said to have accounted for a quantity of approximately seven pounds per month at one period of his life, a consumption which increased rather than grew less as his age advanced and which reached its peak in his final days of imprisonment on St. Helena. A snuff-box accompanied him wherever he went and throughout his life he acquired so many of them that it has been said that could they all be got together and arranged in the order of their acquisition they would make a reliable pictorial chronicle of the chief events and changes in his career.

Under Napoleon the making of snuff-boxes in Paris and other French cities became again an important and prosperous business. As in other countries gold and finely decorated boxes for snuff were the most usual forms of reward given to diplomatic and military dignitaries, or used as bribes for ambiguous services performed by ministers and others whose rank placed them above the acceptance of cash, but not of its equivalent. That some of the latter class were noted as having cost the exchequer of a country to whom they had proved helpful as many as three or more snuff-boxes is a fact noted by Count Corti. The same authority is among those who have recorded details of some of the more noteworthy personal snuff-boxes owned and used by Napoleon. One to which he was so much attached that he was filled with superstitious dread of the results of damaging or losing it, bore upon its lid a miniature portrait of Josephine: this he carried during his Italian campaign, anticipating fatal consequences when the precious lid was found to have been broken. Ultimately this box was lost altogether but replaced by Josephine with another in which was framed a lock of her hair. Other snuff-boxes associated with Napoleon's personal history included one commemorating his marriage to Marie Louise and bearing her miniature, which was presented to him in Austria, and another painted by Isabey with a portrait of the infant King of Rome. For the rest Bonaparte's taste in snuff-boxes often disclosed something of his character, for he owned and caused to be made many that were decorated with medallions or miniature representations of the historic celebrities he most admired. Nearly all these heroes were rulers of nations or leaders of successful armies, among them Alexander the Great, Frederick the Great, Peter the Great and Charles XII of Sweden, while from ancient history were chosen such men as Antiochus and Mithridates.

Gold was the basic material of the majority of exquisitely made boxes of this kind, though it is recorded —again by Count Corti—that another favourite box of Napoleon's, on which appeared the heads of Pompey, Cæsar, Regulus and Sulla wrought in silver, was of tortoise-shell. Usually of gold, enamelled or jewelled, are surviving snuff-boxes bearing the initial 'N' which are assumed to have been made as gifts from Bonaparte. Lacking, however, are details of the appearance of the box with which an attempt was made to murder Napoleon during the time of his First Consulship. The story of the attempt and its frustration is one retailed for the first time in the memoirs of his valet: it tells of the employment of

H

decorators to work on the house occupied by Bonaparte at Malmaison, and of the finding on his desk, after the men's departure, of a box of snuff exactly resembling the one he used at that time. Suspicion was aroused by the fact that it was unlike Napoleon's usual habit to leave a snuff-box in this position; a test was made and the snuff was found to contain poison. French history records more than one such incident, in which snuff and snuff-boxes were the chosen means administering drugs or poison. During the Revolution one of the fruitless efforts made to effect the escape of Marie Antoinette from her imprisonment in the Temple and her ultimate execution had hinged on using a box of drugged snuff as a means of incapacitating a gaoler, a man whose love of Spanish snuff had been noted as his principal weakness.

Tortoise-shell and ivory are perhaps the snuff-box materials which should rank next in importance to gold, since they also were chosen to enclose the finer blends of snuff of former times and to be carried in the more exclusive pockets. Fine tortoise-shell or ivory boxes, indeed, often incorporate gold in decoration, framework or as an alternative to silver for hinges. Well suited to the purpose by reason of its lightness and the good condition in which it preserves snuff, tortoise-shell of all shades of colour from cloudy black to transparent gold was used by eighteenth-century snuff-box makers in England, France, Holland, Russia and other countries. Boxes fashioned entirely of tortoise-shell except for hinges and applied ornamentation of metal were as popular as were top and bottom panels of tortoise-shell in varying shapes set in frameworks of gold, silver, silver-gilt or Sheffield plate. Gems of fine workmanship are to be found in tortoise-shell top panels bearing *piqué*, incrusted or inlaid designs in gold, silver or mother-of-pearl, occasionally of English origin, but more often from the hands of Continental craftsmen. Notable among distinctively English types are the many tortoise-shell boxes embossed with the features of British sovereigns as lid decorations. Some of the finest of these were the work of John Obrisset, an important snuff-box maker of Queen Anne's time, who reproduced on tortoise-shell accepted portraits of the ruling sovereign as well as of Charles I, James I and Queen Elizabeth. After Obrisset's time the four Georges were portrayed in the same way, the head and shoulders carved or impressed directly on tortoise-shell or carried out in *repoussé* silver or gold plates affixed to shell boxes which most frequently are oval in shape. Until well into the nineteenth century Queen Anne's head continued to be reproduced on boxes copied from those made during her reign.

Ivory snuff-boxes were made in forms almost as numerous as those of tortoise-shell and with similar goldsmith's and silversmith's work applied to them. Ivory, too, is one of the materials which was used by the old makers of pocket snuff-rasps and of graters incorporated in boxes, a purpose for which only the harder substances were suitable. The most distinguished and valued of ivory boxes, however, must be counted those bearing fine miniature paintings on their lids, particularly portrait miniatures ascribed to Richard Cosway.

It has been affirmed of Cosway, who worked during the great days of fashionable snuffing in the later part of the eighteenth century and the earlier years of the nineteenth, that his miniature portraits painted on snuff-boxes at the behest of goldsmiths founded his reputation as the most popular miniaturist of his day; from limning on the smooth tops of ivory boxes it was but a step to the adoption of ivory as the most suitable surface for miniature portraiture, an art deriving from the illuminating of manuscripts and originally practised on parchment. Apart from his miniature painting and other work in oil and water colour, Cosway figures in the London history of his time as a collector of Old Master paintings and as an associate of George IV when Prince of Wales, whose frequent visits at the artist's house at one period were scandalously attributed rather less to an interest in painting than to an interest in the beautiful Mrs. Cosway. Be that as it may, there is every likelihood that it was Cosway's work on snuff-boxes which first attracted to him the notice and patronage of the Prince, in the history of whose career the snuff-box is an object of such frequent mention. Even at the time of his coronation snuff-boxes were able to make a not insignificant appearance in the total list of the occasion's expenses, when boxes given away to visiting foreigners and others were charged at a sum exceeding £8,000.

Panels of various kinds of decorated porcelain not infrequently appear instead of tortoise-shell or ivory in presentation and other elaborate boxes, though it is questionable whether many of the more delicate trifles of this kind which are preserved in collections of fine ceramics were ever put to, or intended for, serious use as snuff-carriers. Occasionally used as tops and bottoms in equally pretentious but more substantial boxes were solid ovals or circles of such minerals as rock crystal, agate, bloodstone and cornelian; either smoothly polished or carved; sometimes even inset with smaller stones; and mounted in gold or one of its substitutes, silver, silver-gilt or pinchbeck.

Snuff-boxes made entirely or principally of silver probably outnumber those of the more costly materials so far referred to in a proportion of something like a hundred to one. Silversmiths of most snuff-taking countries have turned out appropriate boxes in a profusion of shapes and sizes, with innumerable forms of decoration, at every period since snuff was introduced. English, Irish and Scotch hall-marks, however, appear on the majority of the best silver boxes surviving in this country from the eighteenth and nineteenth centuries, while French boxes must be counted the most numerous among those of foreign origin. Reference to any large collection of snuff-boxes will show how silver, more than any other material, was employed in making boxes for snuffers of every class and degree, from those whose needs were met by simple little unembellished oblong or oval caskets (made and sold inexpensively enough in Georgian and Victorian times) to the highest in the land, for whom magnificently finished works of the silversmith's art were prepared. On silver boxes of the latter kind *repoussé*, chased and carved decorations are as usual as on those of gold, engraved coats of arms are common, and the former popularity of the silver snuff-box for presentation is testified to by the number which bear commemorative inscriptions.

Only inspection of a representative assembly of such boxes can give an adequate idea of the diversity of types that have been devised since the earliest days of snuffing. Fortunately the numbers in which fine old silver snuff-boxes survive ensure that they are well represented in many museums. The Victoria and Albert Museum, for instance, exhibits a collection of boxes which date from the seventeenth century and extend into the earlier years of the nineteenth. Here are represented many of the commoner forms of snuff-box designed and produced by English silversmiths, from the plain oval bearing engraved arms and a London hall-mark of 1656 to equally simple boxes of nearly two centuries later. With them are fine specimens of rarer designs. Among these a mid-eighteenth century boat-shaped box with twin lids opening side by side to a divided interior, allowing for the carrying of two varieties of snuff; another of long narrow shape, made to contain a snuff-rasp in about the year 1700; one having almost the form of a small spectacle-case, with the base of tortoise-shell; several bearing the features of King Charles or Queen Anne on tortoise-shell lids, but otherwise fashioned from silver; an Irish box, round in shape, of the end of the eighteenth century; and, made in George III's latter years, a silver-gilt 'snuff' incorporating a musical-box.

Historical associations belong to some of the silver boxes in the same collection. Of early date is a little box which unmistakably suggests in its shape and size that it was intended for snuff rather than for any of the other purposes for which pocket boxes were made at the period; it is of octagonal formation with its lid cast and chased in a relief design imitating Chinese work, and is inscribed: 'The gift of K. Charles II to Mrs Gwin; Her Son Charles, Duke of St. Albans Gave this to me Lawrance Answorth 1720 who had then the Honour to be Head Butler To Him'.

As intriguing as the box given to Nell Gwyn by the King and inherited by their only son to survive childhood, is one of silver-gilt, set with oak taken from H.M.S. *Bellerophon*, which is in the form of a hollowed mask of Nelson's features. This bears the words and date: 'Nile, St. Vincent, Calvir, Copenhagen, Trafalgar. Oct. 21. 1805'.

In most noteworthy snuff-box collections are to be found examples of the silver-mounted shells which were once so much in vogue. Nearly always they take the same form: that of a stag cowrie cut off flat on the side of its natural opening and fitted with a hinged silver lid. Like tortoise-shell, these cowries were found to be admirable retainers of snuff's freshness and savour. Their lids generally were perfectly contrived to make them almost airtight, and on them are found hall-marks of the last years of the seventeenth century and the first of the eighteenth, while armorial engraving occurs frequently enough to point to their having been prized possessions of men of wealth.

For the rest old silver snuff-boxes are confined to no bounds of form or type but are to be met with in a multiformity that compels admiration for their designers. Recent years have seen interest in them increase to an extent that has made a fine specimen a highly priced and easily saleable 'antique' in the hands of a curio-dealer who not long since would have considered it a drug to be disposed of with difficulty for a few shillings. Neither collectors nor snuff-takers are responsible for this demand; the cause is to be looked for in modern uses for snuff-boxes, among them that of a cigarette-container. It is a fact that a sound and well-finished old silver snuff of dimensions which will allow it to be used as a cigarette-case commands a price of double as much as can be asked for one that is similar but a fraction of an inch too short for this purpose. Very small boxes, on the other hand, are sought for as containers of such aids to present-day existence as aspirin and saccharine tablets, notwithstanding the destructive effect of their hardness on the fine gilding with which most old silver snuff-boxes are lined.

There can be few kinds of wood, British-grown or imported, that have not been used in the manufacture of snuff-boxes. George IV, on making a visit to Scotland not long after his coronation, was presented with a snuff-box composed of the woods of memorable trees commemorated in Scottish songs and ballads—among many the Elderslie Yew, Torwood Oak, Birk of Invermay, Bush aboon Traquair, Cruikston Yew and Broom of Cowdenknowes. The base of this elaborate example of the lengths to which snuff-box making could be carried was decorated in appropriate taste with a transcription of the tune of *Auld Lang Syne*. A completely comprehensive survey of wooden snuff-boxes would cover others as remarkable, side by side with the simplest, cheapest type of snuff-container made of roughly glued-together sections of deal, such as had its place in every pedlar's pack a century and a half ago and was commonly sold for a few pence. Figuring between these two extremes would be imported curiosities like those that came from South America in the seventeenth century, quaintly carved and fashioned from unidentified nut-woods of an iron hardness; boxes made in Britain from a score of kinds of foreign woods, mahogany and ebony among them; and those of the timber of every home-grown tree from oak to the various orchard fruit-bearers.

The shapes and designs of snuff-boxes of wood are more diverse than is found in other materials, since amateur makers, carvers and country craftsmen were wont to carry out their ideas in odd, left-over pieces of wood which were too small for almost any other purpose than a snuff-box, and numbers of their quaint and original productions survive among the quantities of standardised boxes. Every vagary of personal or professional taste could be said to be exemplified in wooden snuffs for the pocket or the table. Carved portrait heads of famous characters or unknown persons (sometimes, no doubt, depicting the box's original owner) made a popular form of box when hollowed out and fitted with a removable top or hinged opening at the back. Members of certain trades had a weakness for miniature models of articles appropriate to their callings: tiny hardwood casks, hooped with silver, brass or even gold, were made for publicans and brewers; the hollowed model of a fox's mask or a horse's hoof made its appeal to the huntsman or the coachman; it may be assumed that shoe-makers were the best customers for the rosewood and mahogany table boxes which, early in the last century, were fashioned in fair numbers in the shape of a boot, with a neatly sliding lid at the top and the outline of the sole, heel and fastening delicately picked out with minute brass nails; while Mr. Sowerberry, to whom Oliver

IX Wooden Snuff-boxes

A Table Box in form of a shoe, sliding lid. Three Laurencekirk Boxes, hinged lids. A Round Box, detachable lid bearing hunting scene in relief

X Papier Mâché Snuff-boxes

Two Table Boxes, detachable lids decorated with sporting scenes in colour. Pocket Box in form of a horse's hoof, hinged lid. Oblong 'Potato Skin' Box for the pocket, hinged lid painted with a

Twist was bound apprentice, almost certainly was not the only undertaker to carry his snuff in 'an ingenious little model of a patent coffin'.

Since nothing is more important in a pocket snuff-box than that its lid should fit closely and shut tightly enough to permit neither the escape of snuff nor the entrance of unnecessary air, it is surprising how many old examples —even some of those that were made less than a century ago—fail in this respect. Nearly always the worst equipped are boxes with hinged lids. The commonest type of round box having an unattached top, removed and replaced by a twist of the fingers, could be made virtually airtight by precise turning, and almost as close sealing was provided in oval boxes having simple grooves cut in their edges, but hinges presented a problem which the worker in wood and similar substances took longer to overcome than did the maker of metal boxes. Though many attempts were made to design a wooden hinge which would not become clogged by snuff-dust and would exclude the air, few if any efficiently hinged wooden snuffs are of earlier date than the end of the eighteenth century, when the first of the so-called Laurencekirk boxes appeared in Scotland, later to become rapidly accepted and much copied.

Usually made of plane-tree wood, and more often oblong than any other shape, boxes of this kind were effective in use, cheap to make, and lent themselves to several forms of outward decoration. Chief among their virtues, however, was the ingeniously neat hinge, having the appearance of being entirely of wood and being almost invisible with the lid closed. In fact the hinge was composed of a fine brass pin completely encased within a series of little wooden rollers meeting one another so exactly as to exclude the finest snuff grains from their joints. Generally these rollers are found to be seven in number: four of them—including the two endmost—being rigid and cut from the back of the box's body; and three turning on the pin and forming part of the lid. As exactly cut as the rollers, the projecting under-side of the lid fits down into the well of the box to complete a perfect closure.

Laurencekirk boxes belong to the number of successful inventions that have brought little profit to their origin-ators and much to their later manufacturers and others able to exploit them. Not long after the first few of the ingeniously jointed little boxes had been made, in the Kincardineshire village whose name was given to them, they had achieved a local reputation; soon, the making of them became a local industry, which later developed widely and extremely profitably when snuff-takers and snuff-boxers (as retail sellers of snuff-boxes were called) all over Britain came to realise their merits.

The tale of the Laurencekirk box's origin and success, and of the remarkable man who was its inventor, rests mainly on brief statements made by two or three con-tributors to old miscellanies. On some points the evidence given in different records is conflicting, though in general terms agreeing closely enough to amount to a reasonably connected narrative.

The whole credit for the ingenious hinge and the general design of the Laurencekirk type of box should be given to James Sandy, whose now almost forgotten accomplishments and achievements in the face of personal misfortune earned him, during his lifetime and soon after his death, such descriptions as, 'a genius and eccentric character rarely surpassed', whose 'talent for practical mechanics was universal'. Early in life, and while living at Laurencekirk, Sandy entirely lost the use of his legs, and thereafter faced with cheerfulness and resignation a lifetime of confinement to his bed. From the first he determined to make his affliction as tolerable as circumstances would permit by occupying himself both usefully and profitably with his hands. He began by designing and causing to be made an extraordinary piece of furniture which should serve him both as a bed and a workshop. This was described as 'a kind of circular bed, the sides of which, being raised about 18 inches above the clothes, were employed as a platform for turning-lathes, vices and cases for tools of all kinds'. Propped up in his strange couch, Sandy worked in wood, metal and even glass; making objects of his own invention or design; improving on the ideas and productions of other craftsmen; and showing himself able to repair or put into working order almost any mechanical contrivance of small size. Nearly all the tools he used were of his own making; some of them, among them those employed in fashioning the snuff-box hinges, of a kind previously unknown.

The wooden-jointed snuff-box was but one of many cleverly contrived and skilfully finished pieces of work which first took shape in Sandy's bedroom workshop. During his years of enforced confinement his always active brain and deft fingers developed an ever increasing ability, until it seemed to his friends that his skill was almost uncanny. Wooden objects of his making were at first limited to small pieces but in time he was able to produce furniture of considerable size, including certain tables which were described as 'very curious'. From repairing clocks, he progressed to making them. Musical instruments of more than one kind entirely designed and constructed on the bed-bench were spoken of as possessing both an elegant finish and a sweet tone. Reflecting telescopes and other optical instruments of Sandy's contriving were found to be equally perfect and practical. The actual spinning of flax may or may not have been beyond his resources, but it is on record that he thought out and suggested certain improvements in the machinery for this purpose which were adopted and found valuable by manufacturers of linen. A natural gift for drawing enabled Sandy to make preliminary sketches and designs of his more ambitious mechanical inventions and devices. He also acquired—as always, by self-teaching—the art of engraving on copper and other metals.

One more of his varied interests perhaps should be remembered since it helps to substantiate his reputation for eccentricity. Birds, it appears, and the habits of birds were subjects he managed to study and derive great pleasure from, notwithstanding his remaining always in one room. As he could not observe wild birds in their natural surroundings he decided to rear them at home, by means of hatching out under his bedclothes the eggs he persuaded his friends to collect and bring to him. The results were varied and wonderful. The strange room became an aviary as well as a workshop, wherein Sandy 'reared various broods with the tenderness of a parent'. Education followed production, and in due course such pupils as proved amenable were taught to sing in a manner agreeable to the master's taste.

The number of visitors at the inventor's home increased considerably when it became known in the district that they might be entertained by the sight of assorted wild birds perched on the host's head and bedclothes, and by the sound of their concerted and unnatural warbling. At no time, however had James Sandy been neglected or left long without company, his naturally cheerful disposition having made him popular with his neighbours. His active mind, too, insured his being consulted on all matters of moment and the acceptance of his opinions with respect; his room, in fact, was treated as something of a village gathering place where people were wont to drop in for a gossip at all hours of the day and 'where the affairs of church and state were freely discussed'. For the rest, he has been described as a man enjoying good health and a strong constitution except for the uselessness of his lower limbs; in appearance he had become pale and wan from his years of confinement, but was bright and amiable of expression.

In all, Sandy stayed in bed for upwards of half a century, keeping himself busy and amused for almost the whole of that time. One of his biographers maintained that only on three occasions was he known to leave his bed, and then only because his house was either flooded or thought to be on fire. This statement, however, does not fit in with another: that Sandy's home—in later years, at any rate—was at Alyth, in Perthshire, to which place at some time he must have travelled from Laurencekirk. The final distinction of an otherwise not unremarkable career was his decision to make a tardy marriage: the wedding took place some three weeks before his death.

An altogether fitting and proper sequel to the story tells of the widow inheriting a considerable property, her husband's 'ingenuity and industry having brought him a comfortable and honourable independence'. This is the version endorsed by William Hone and that which one would prefer to believe. Unhappily, one John M'Diarmid, a local, contemporary and possibly well-informed writer, published a very different opinion, handed on in later years by John Timbs, to the effect that our inventor 'died, as he had lived, in the lowest poverty'.

Whatever may have been his true circumstances, there seems to be little doubt that Sandy reaped but little financial gain, in proportion to the fortunes made by others, from the Laurencekirk box, by far the most important of his inventions. Unable to foresee the possibilities of the idea, he neither patented it nor bothered to keep it to himself. One of the first of his acquaintances to be put in possession of the secret of making both the jointed hinges and the peculiar tools that were needed was a local carpenter, who forthwith set about producing Laurencekirk boxes in considerable numbers and selling them at enormous profit to himself. Within a few years an ever-extending demand for his products had made the enterprising joiner a rich man.

Other makers followed his example when they had contrived to provide themselves with suitable tools. The making of boxes very much resembling Sandy's originals became a considerable Scottish industry in which several opposition workshops were engaged, the workmen in each of them being sworn not to divulge to others the 'secret' nature of the tools they were using. One of the most successful manufacturers was one Crawford, of Cumnock in Ayrshire, who, early in the nineteenth century employed a craftsman who had been a watch-maker to make the tools, and then built up a trade in the boxes which eventually earned him between £7,000 and £8,000 a year. The whole district benefited from Crawford's prosperity since he employed a great deal of local labour; labour, in fact, accounted for almost the whole of his overhead expenses, the cost of the materials used being practically negligible. Though eventually, as competition increased, the prices charged for Laurence-kirk type boxes became reasonable enough, in the earlier years of their popularity the charge for a single snuff-box was two-and-a-half guineas, and that for a lady's work-box made on the same principle as much as £25. The value of the plane wood used in a snuff-box was estimated at one penny, and twopence easily covered the cost of varnish and other liquids needed for finishing and decoration. Authority states that twenty-five shillings worth of plane tree wood converted into snuff-boxes could be made to yield £3,000.

The best of the surviving boxes of this kind, however, do suggest that the workers employed in their making were highly skilled and painstaking. Each box was cut from solid wood and put together in but two pieces, joined only at the hinge. Thin wooden walls alone were found to allow snuff to dry very quickly, so that a lining was necessary; nearly always it was a neatly applied skin of lead paper, rather like that found in old wooden tea-caddies. Outward decoration was of a number of kinds.

Rarest and most valuable of Laurencekirk boxes are the few that, being sold plain or afterwards rubbed down to a plain surface, fell into the hands of artists whose work is distinctive and recognisable and who painted miniature scenes on the lids, and occasionally the sides as well. One or two of the better known English sporting painters of the first half of the last century were among those who once in a way would embellish a wooden snuff, probably as a gift for a friend or patron, with a hunting scene or a tiny portrait of a favourite horse. One known and very fine example is a Laurencekirk box bearing on each of its six surfaces a miniature sporting painting that is clearly from the brush of the elder Henry Alken, certainly the most versatile, and in many ways one of the most gifted, of the illustrators of sport.

The majority of Laurencekirk and similar boxes were sent out by the makers finished with a simple decoration protected by a coat or two of varnish. Many of the lids bear illustrations of buildings of contemporary interest, like Carlton House, the Royal Pavilion at Brighton, or one of London's Regency churches. Scenes from Æsop's *Fables* are found occasionally, but more often ships at sea, sporting subjects, or neat little representations of carriages of different kinds and mail and stage coaches on the road. As a rule these designs are entirely in black on the plain wood; red, or at the most one other colour, was sometimes introduced. A black floral or geometrical design usually encloses the lid-picture, and is repeated on the sides, ends and bottom of the box. Exceptionally, work of this kind was carried out by direct etching; commonly, by printing in the manner of the decorators of china and tiles. The tops of the boxes are seldom so flat as to have permitted direct printing from a copper plate, but their slightly curved, perfectly smooth surfaces were admirably suited to printing from a paper transfer.

Beautifully defined results without a hint of smudginess could be obtained by this method of printing, which had been brought to a fine art by the time the Scotch jointed snuff-boxes were at the height of their popularity. It was then an art more than half a century old, having been discovered in or about the year 1749. The discovery was made quite accidentally by John Sadler, a Liverpool engraver, while working at home in a room in which his children were playing. He had thrown on the floor an unsatisfactory proof of an engraving; while the ink was still wet, one of the children picked up the proof, pressed it against the side of an earthenware mug, and delightedly showed his father how 'the picture came off'. Unlike poor Sandy, Sadler knew a valuable idea when he met one; he experimented and improved until, in a few years time, he was able to declare upon oath that he and one other man:

> Without the aid or assistance of any other person or persons, did, within the space of six hours, print upwards of 1,200 earthen tiles, more in number and better and neater than one hundred skilful pot-painters could have painted in the common and usual way of painting with a pencil.

Subsequently the transfer-printing process was developed to an endless extent for the adornment of pottery, china, enamels and many smooth-surfaced objects of the snuff-box order, fine examples of the Laurencekirk kind proving how successfully it could be applied to wood.

Perhaps the commonest and most generally popular of all the forms of decoration used by Scottish snuff-box makers was chequer-work, at its simplest and neatest a pattern of very finely marked cross-hatched lines in black, and at its most elaborate and ornate a highly coloured tartan. All the lines were drawn separately on the wood by means of pens fixed in a ruling-machine. In Victorian times boxes were made in all the principal clan tartans, correctly coloured, and in a variety of less spectacular plaid patterns. Particularly associated with these boxes was the firm of Smith of Mauchline, whose products—as well as those of other makers—became very generally known among snuff-boxers in England, and in later years among antique dealers, as 'Muchlin boxes'.

Today, collectors have more difficulty in finding good examples of old jointed wooden boxes than snuffs of almost any other kind. The hinges, the principal virtue of the boxes, have proved to be their main weakness, their rollers snapping very easily as the wood dried with age. The lead-paper linings, too, usually are found to be perished in boxes made a century or more ago. While re-lining with a similar material is fairly simple, little or nothing can be done toward repairing a box fractured at its wooden hinge-casing.

Only rarely are boxes of the Laurencekirk or Muchlin description found to be lined with hard, imperishable substances. More often tortoise-shell, gold, or silver was used to line the finer round and oval wooden snuffs made with lift-off lids, either for the pocket or the table. An example is the gold-lined amboyna wood box mentioned in an earlier chapter as having been presented to George Evans by Lord Petersham, who personally designed and caused to be made numbers of the magnificent boxes given to his acquaintances or intended for his own famous collection, which—incidentally—was valued at £3,000. Expensive linings generally go with unusual woods, either smoothly polished to exhibit the full beauty of an exceptional grain or bearing designs that

I

may be carved or impressed; the latter being sometimes elaborate miniature scenes inspired by contemporary painters. Exceptionally, certain finely made wooden boxes of the costlier kind, outwardly embellished with silver or gold inlay, were fitted with an inner casing of one of the cheaper metals, like brass or copper. Table boxes more often are of this description than those for the pocket, and among their number are such rarities as spoon-snuffs, hinged with the same metal that lines the well and lid, and closing in much the same way as a mustard-pot with a little incision allowing the handle of a snuff-spoon to project.

Unlined wood boxes seldom prove to be a success, snuff kept in them becoming, dry, gritty and savourless in a very short time. Noticeably most of those that were made in days when every purchaser of one was a critical and experienced snuff-taker were unprovided with linings for some good reason. Either they were of such a shape that it was impossible to fit them with an effective inner casing—like the carved portrait-mask boxes, and those in the form of a shoe—or else they were fashioned from hard, smooth, ivory-like woods, often scooped out of solid pieces and purposely left with very thick walls. Thin, light-weight wood snuff-boxes nearly always were lined.

One of the great virtues of papier mâché snuff-boxes, which at first shared and eventually usurped the popularity of those of wood, was that they needed no lining. Of all the cheaper materials of which snuff-boxes were —and still are—made, papier mâché in fact was considered the most suitable for the purpose, and it is probable that papier mâché snuffs have been turned out in greater numbers than any other kind. Authority describes papier mâché as a substance composed of paper pulp, often mixed with other materials, which can be moulded into varied shapes and is made, by a peculiar treatment, to resemble varnished or lacquered wood. In spite of its name, there is no good reason for supposing that the composition had a French origin. Quantities of papier mâché boxes for snuff were made in Britain, as well, no doubt, as in other countries, early in the nineteenth century. During the first part of Queen Victoria's reign the market for them was a wide one among the poorer class of snuff-takers, and their manufacture represented a considerable part of a papier mâché industry producing numberless domestic objects, varying in size from buttons and thimble-cases to chairs, tables and even larger pieces of furniture. A modest demand for papier mâché snuff-boxes continues in the present day and many tobacconists still sell them; as a rule modern ones are plain black with lids carrying some slight form of decoration like a gilt border or a pattern made up of inset pieces of mother-of-pearl.

Both these means of ornamenting papier mâché date from days when snuff-boxes were in wide demand. Victorian boxes with their tops bordered with gilt garlands or Greek key-patterns, often encircling mottoes or gift messages in gilt letters, were popular as presents and keepsakes. Commoner still were those inlaid with mother-of-pearl: at their simplest, having no more than a single diamond-shaped or oval piece of pearl—on which initials could be scratched—let into the lid; at their most elaborate, carrying a mosaic design or even a view of some noted beauty spot made up of many chips of mother-of-pearl of contrasting shades.

Papier mâché lent itself to decoration of a number of kinds. To the painter in miniature the silk-smooth surface proved a good ground for oil paint. Old papier mâché snuffs much more often than wooden ones bear original paintings, varying as much in merit as they do in subject. The work of an artist of importance may be suspected only occasionally, still more rarely proved, and any form of signature, even an initial, is unusual; but capable copies of their better known themes are fairly plentiful. Portrait, landscape, seascape, and caricature subjects were all popular; portraits of members of the Royal family and contemporary celebrities appear as frequently on the tops of papier mâché snuffs as do the features of imaginary beauties; Trafalgar, Waterloo and other battles on sea and land are as well represented as peaceful rural scenes; and nearly every branch of sport and pastime, from cricket and cockfighting to hunting and racing, has been illustrated in the same way.

Though many of the painters of box lids were struggling artists glad enough to earn a few shillings by working for snuff-boxers and manufacturers, their products were too costly for the average purchaser. Popular demand for something cheaper was met by illustrating papier mâché boxes with prints affixed to their lids. Whatever means were used to make paper adhere to the surface was a perfect one, and seldom is one found to have peeled or rubbed loose at the edges even on boxes that are considerably more than a hundred years old. Plain prints in black line were used on the cheapest boxes, and good impressions in colour on others; some were finished by over-painting in oils, making so perfect an appearance when varnished as to be easily and quite often mistaken for original paintings.

The use of prints for snuff-box decorations provided the widest choice of subjects and allowed those that proved most popular to be reproduced to an almost unlimited extent. Every snuff-boxer was able to keep in stock a varied selection of boxes with the kind of picture tops most likely to suit the taste of his customers, and with prices equally to their taste. Oblong and oval hinged boxes for pocket use which bore simple, uncoloured portrait or caricature prints were sold in London shops in the eighteen-twenties for a shilling or less. Ten times

as much might be asked for a circular table snuff of
papier mâché on the lift-off lid of which was a little
masterpiece printed or painted in full colour and exactly
reproducing in miniature some popular sporting aquatint
of the period; perhaps a well-known coaching scene after
James Pollard, or a portrait of the previous year's Derby
winner copied from a full-sized print after J. F. Herring.
Changing fashions can be observed in pictorial snuff-
boxes, as in clothes and furniture and other intimate
things. Notable are the numbers of boxes made in the
first years of the reign of Victoria, and originally sold at
high prices, carrying a portrait of the young Queen, and
those of a little later that display the uniformed figure of
the Prince Consort.

Separated by at least a paragraph from boxes made to
gratify loyal, sporting, or otherwise respectable tastes
should be a note on lid decorations which at the best
were vulgar and at the worst indecent. A considerable
trade was carried on in wares of this kind, most of them
made of papier mâché. De Morgan, writing in the
eighteen-seventies, mentioned that:

'Fifty years ago a fashionable snuff-boxer would be
under inducement to have a stock with very objectionable
pictures.'

Much later than the date suggested such boxes were
still being made, both in small sizes for snuff and larger for
tobacco when the popularity of snuffing was declining.
Their vendors in London included not only 'fashionable
snuff-boxers' and minor tobacconists but a number of
itinerant hawkers and street pedlars.

Many connoisseurs of snuff maintained that papier
mâché preserved freshness and flavour better than any
substance of which boxes were made. Unlike metals and
some other materials it became neither very hot nor
unduly cold in use, thus keeping snuff at an equable
warmth. The temperature of good snuff was considered

as important as that of good wine; its *bouquet*, like that of brandy, burgundy and claret, was best appreciated when brought out by slight warmth, which could be maintained in a papier mâché box by carrying it in the waistcoat pocket during the day and putting it under the pillow at night. One authority of George IV's time who had been a life-long snuff-taker no doubt expressed the preference of many of his contemporaries when he wrote: 'A silver snuff-box and I parted company years ago. My customary boxes have been papier mâché, plain black.'

Particularly esteemed was a type of papier mâché made from potato skins, which would keep snuff fresh and moist longer than the common kind. Potato boxes, as they were called, may be distinguished by their peculiar lacquer finish of a greenish tinge, generally flecked with gold or red streaks looking rather like sealing-wax. Extremely strong, old boxes of this material seldom if ever are found to have cracked or warped.

The principal failing of papier mâché snuffs, and the only essential in which they were inferior to those of wood, was their closing. Instead of the neat roller hinge of the Laurencekirk lid, an exposed and rather clumsy brass affair, very apt to become clogged with snuff, was fitted to most papier mâché pocket boxes. Nor were the table boxes, usually round in shape, provided with such closely fitting tops as were the best of the wooden ones.

Though the works of a number of authorities on glass may be searched in vain for reference to old glass snuff-boxes there can be little doubt that some of the smaller two-piece jars and covered boxes made at English and Irish manufactories of the past were intended and used as table snuff-containers. Some of these are of cut glass of the kind that came from Belfast and Londonderry; rarely they have that highly prized slightly blue tint which suggests that they were made at Waterford, where glass production began when fashionable snuff-taking was at its height in the last quarter of the eighteenth century. Snuff, however, unlike wine, does not look at its best when seen through fine transparent glass; more suitable were the opaque and coloured glasses for which Bristol and its near neighbour Nailsea had become famous at about the same period: particularly the enamel glass first made at Bristol as a substitute for imported porcelain; the rich dark blue glass with gilt decorations from the same source; and marbled glass from Nailsea.

Glass, also, was one of the two materials from which were made the most delicate of Chinese snuff-bottles, the other being fine china. Though it is most unlikely that many people in Britain used these trifles for carrying snuff, as the Chinese did, the numbers of them seen in this country suggest that they have been imported in fair quantities as curiosities and ornaments. They are of varied shapes but in size generally small enough to fit easily into a waistcoat pocket. Those of glass sometimes bear decorations miraculously painted on the *inside*; those of china are of a number of wares, periods and patterns. A little spoon was an essential to snuff-taking in China and the stoppers of many bottles were made with the spoon as an attachment, in the manner of a medicine-bottle dipper, just long enough to reach the bottom. Especially pleasing are bottles which were imported in an unfinished state and later were fitted with stoppers and hinged caps of English silver bearing Georgian hall-marks.

Enamel may be represented in large and important snuff-box collections by several kinds of fine foreign products as well as by English boxes, the latter, however, heavily outnumbering the former. Elsewhere—in the cabinets and curio tables of the more modest collectors, in provincial museums, and in antique dealers' shops—boxes of the Battersea kind, genuine or allegedly genuine, prove most numerous and popular among enamels. Real

Battersea enamel boxes are little works of art with an irresistible appeal to the connoisseur of fine things, and were made at a factory which began operations half way through the eighteenth century at York House, Battersea. Here transfer-printing, soon after its origin in Liverpool, was one of the means employed to decorate white or coloured enamel objects of many kinds, from cups and saucers to candlesticks. Snuffs were among the several sorts of boxes produced, along with those for patches, comfits, *bonbons*, thimbles and so on; suitable metal hinges and fastenings and appropriate shapes distinguishing the snuffs from the others, some of them fashioned in the forms of birds, with plumage neatly coloured, or the heads of dogs or foxes with inset glass eyes.

All are commonly covered by the much misused term 'Battersea snuff-boxes'. In fact, the majority of boxes so described are neither from Battersea nor for snuff. The success of the London manufactory inspired the usual imitators, the most notable and one of the first of whom was a certain George Brett, of Bilston, the originator of a considerable Staffordshire industry in enamels, principally boxes. Bilston boxes were made in far greater numbers than those of Battersea and of somewhat inferior quality. Few of them bear transfer-printed scenes as decorations or are of original shapes; the most numerous are little pink or blue boxes, oval or rectangular, with white lids on which appear printed messages or mottoes and modest designs in black or one colour; many were made for sale as souvenirs to visitors at spas and cathedral cities and are appropriately embellished: 'A Trifle from Bath' or 'A Present from York'. Some no doubt were used for snuff, but unsuitable hinges and the presence of little mirrors inside the lids of many of them suggest other uses. Even more than most popular and saleable collectors' pieces have Battersea and Bilston boxes been reproduced in modern times, and the wholesale diffusion

XI Horn Snuff-box in form of Napoleon's Hat

One of the *Tabatières au petit chapeau* made during the Napoleonic
Wars. Hinged side decorated with battle scene, Napoleon at Toulon,
in relief

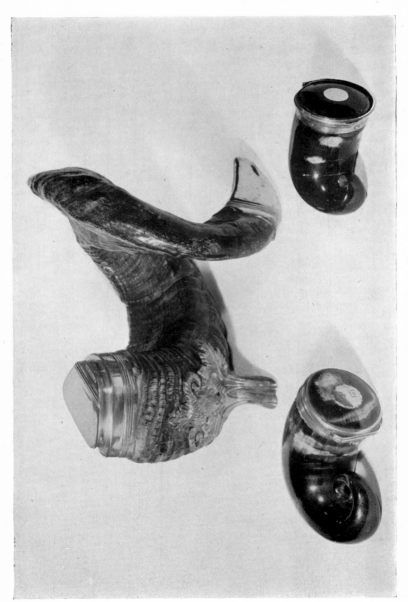

XII Scottish Mulls

Silver-mounted Horns, the largest a Table Mull

of fakes has made them risky things to acquire without expert knowledge.

Earlier passing mention has been made of pinchbeck and Sheffield plate as having been employed by snuff-box makers. Both are found combined with substances like tortoise-shell and mother-of-pearl and used alone for boxes which, in shapes and decorations, take nearly as many forms as do those of gold and silver. Pinchbeck and Sheffield plate were both products of the snuff-taking age which should be remembered together—the one as a substitute for gold and the other as a counterfeit of silver—among the materials of snuff-boxes that were sold cheaply at the time of their making and which still remain comparatively reasonably priced. Pinchbeck, particularly, may be counted less 'collected' and consequently less expensive than most old substances, and good eighteenth century snuff-boxes of elegant appearance that are still fit to be put to their original use are by no means hard to find. They are part of an immense output of small objects of all kinds, ranging from personal jewellery to table forks, which began in the latter part of the seventeenth century when Christopher Pinchbeck, a London watchmaker, hit upon an economical composite of copper and zinc which could be finished to present a lasting gold-like appearance. For about a hundred years the making of an endless list of decorative articles of pinchbeck continued; Mr Pinchbeck and the son who inherited his manufacturing secret were the blessed benefactors of every pretentious dandy and coffee-house fop unable to afford gold but thus enabled to equip himself at trifling cost with something that looked very like it, until at last the name of pinchbeck became so widely associated with all that was spurious that it was adopted as a general term of contempt. The last was an association which the metal itself did not deserve. As an imitation of gold it was greatly superior to many successors, and pinchbeck snuffs, quizzing-glasses and similar things have often kept for two hundred years and more their original colour.

Though modern interest in, and demand for, Sheffield plate may be greater than is the case with pinchbeck, it centres chiefly on the larger and more important pieces of table plate and such things as teapots and candlesticks. Snuff-boxes were among the smallest objects made in Sheffield plate, the earliest of them dating from very soon after Boulsover's discovery of the plating process in 1742. Copper was the basis of all genuine old plate of this kind, the surface being silver which, in the form of a thin layer, was applied to the copper and fused to it by heat and pressure. The result imitated solid silver in appearance very closely, the depth of the silver skin giving a quality and colour—and the copper a solidity—incomparably superior to the effect produced by the more recent processes of electro-plating; even much worn old pieces showing glimpses of the copper at the edges and most-polished parts have a greater charm for some collectors than has the finest silver of equal date. Many articles of Sheffield plate reproduce the shapes and designs of silver pieces much earlier in date than the time of Boulsover's discovery, some of the snuff-boxes being copies of silver ones of Queen Anne's reign. Notable among the many forms of the Sheffield plate snuff are patterns decorated with a Georgian silver coin set in the centre of the lid. The last, however, is an attractive embellishment—and to the unwary buyer an apparent proof of age—of which full advantage has been taken by the ever active and ingenious faker of the 'antique'.

Of other metal snuff-boxes that once were popular because they cost very little to buy, the principal were those of brass, pewter and copper. Most of the shapes generally favoured by workers in gold and silver were reproduced in workaday metals for the benefit of snuffers who could afford nothing more costly. Decoration, when there was any at all on a box, as a rule was engraved or scratched; more often than those of pewter and copper were rectangular or oval brass snuffs ornamented with *repoussé* patterns or scenes of a simple kind. Old brass boxes may be counted a good deal more numerous than copper or pewter, some of the pocket varieties having forms that are attractive to the collector, particularly those with a curved or boat-shaped well, and a flat top, part of which opens on a hinge. Among the quaintest are those made like a little bellows, with projections to fit the nostrils.

Much more importance attaches to horn boxes, horn having been one of the first, as it was the most continuously used, of all the snuff-containing substances. English horn snuffs alone—excluding for the moment those of Scotland and the many that came to Britain from abroad—might be traced from their beginnings in the seventeenth century through a hundred different forms as far as neat little hinged cases only recently made and still on sale, brand new, in tobacconists' shops. A complete review of their shapes and sizes and the means of improving them would include those of early date having rasps attached to them, or a roughness serving the purpose of a rasp cut on their outer sides, together with Queen Anne ovals, both plain and variously decorated, and many types that were produced in the reigns of the Georges, some few inlaid or even lined with gold or silver. Inevitably such a list, with adequate reference to embossed, carved and applied metal or semi-precious stone decorations, would entail superfluous repetition of details already associated with snuff-boxes made of other materials, particularly tortoise-shell and ivory.

Foreign boxes of horn, imported from a number of different countries, also took many forms. Though little interest except that of age can be claimed for the majority,

some have acquired value and a ready market by reason
of attractive appearance or historical association. Both
these distinctions belong to certain intriguing little snuffs
known to collectors of Napoleonic relics as *Tabatières au
Petit-chapeau*, which once reached England and Ireland
in fair numbers and, though rare enough now, still are
to be met with occasionally. They were made in numbers
in France when Bonaparte was at the height of his power
and triumph, and served both as snuff-boxes and symbols
of loyalty and devotion to thousands of the emperor's
admirers, particularly men who carried arms in his cam-
paigns. All *tabatières au petit-chapeau* are of the shape
which the name implies, that of Napoleon's hat; and
most are of horn, though some were fashioned in metals
or tortoise-shell. Each is contrived so that the curving
side of the hat serves as a well to contain snuff, while
the flat side forms the lid of the box and is neatly hinged
with joints cut from the solid horn and showing no
metal. Outwardly the curved surface is smoothly polished
and embellished only by a minutely perfect cockade
inlaid in bone, coloured red and white and finished in
gold. Sometimes the flat surface of the lid, too, is plain,
but on the best of the *tabatières* it will carry an appropriate portrait or scene in relief; as a rule a reproduction
of a battle picture in which the figure of Napoleon is
prominent, or of one of the better-known portraits of the
Emperor after David or one of his contemporaries.

After the fall of Napoleon it was a danger and an
offence for a Frenchman to be found in possession of one
of the little hat-shaped boxes that so disclosed his sympathies, and it may well be that it was at this time that
so many of them found their way to this country until
death ended any possibility of Bonaparte's regaining
power. As snuff-boxes they are wellnigh perfect, having
a shape that both fits a waistcoat pocket snugly and allows
the last grain of snuff in the scooped-out well to be picked

up between forefinger and thumb, while their lids are so beautifully fitted as to be almost airtight.

Beyond boxes manufactured from horn are snuff-containers contrived from horns allowed to keep their natural or almost natural forms. Within the latter category come those snuffs which consist of a hoof, or more often half the hoof, of some small cloven-footed animal of the deer species. Some of the animals in question must have been very small indeed, since the boxes often provide room for little more than a teaspoonful of snuff. Usually the normal shape of the hoof has been left unchanged except by polishing, and the fitting of a hinged lid which may be either of horn or metal. Most of such boxes probably have a Scottish origin.

Most certainly Scottish are the majority of snuff-mulls which were made from the head horns of several kinds of animals, among them rams, mountain goats and even Highland cattle. The traditional means of carrying snuff in the days when almost every Scot treated snuff as an essential, horn mulls are of remote origin. Scottish literature from the seventeenth century onwards abounds with references to them, sometimes (as is the case in the quotation from the poet Cleland given in Chapter I) in the more logical spelling—mill, more often in the dialect form of mull: a third version of the word, which suggests the origin of a family name, occurs as an early eighteenth-century entry in the Household Book of Lady G. Baillie: 'For 3 snuff milnes £4'. Scott in many relevant passages kept to the colloquialism, as when, in *The Two Drovers*, 'Some thrust out their snuff-mulls for the parting pinch'. Webster, in his *Rhymes* (1835), was more pedantic—and about the nature of the object more explicit—when he wrote, 'His snuff-mill was the horn o' ram'.

Rams' horns probably are the commonest mulls. As a rule they keep something near the original shape of the horn though many have been artificially turned to take two, or even three, twists. The opening, at the wider end, may close with a cork bung capped with horn or wood or it may have a hinged top. Hinged caps generally are silver-mounted horn or solid silver, the more pretentious having been set with an amethyst, cairngorm, agate, topaz or imitation stone. Any part of a mull may bear a silver plate or shield inscribed with a name or initials, and the point may be capped with silver or brass. A very few mulls have the pointed end finished with an ingenious contrivance which, at the turn of a knob, measures and ejects a single but generous pinch of snuff in a little cup from which it could be sniffed. These and some others of the larger kind, such as were made from horns or half-horns of cattle, often have a hole drilled through the small end so that they could be carried slung from a belt or button. While some are six or more inches from end to end and capable of holding several ounces of snuff, the smallest mulls, twisted like little bugles, take up little more room in a pocket and hold little more snuff than a snuff-box made for the waistcoat. Comparatively rare are genuine mulls of the eighteenth century or earlier containing the original spoon—sometimes fastened by a chain—which was a common, but not invariable, accompaniment to snuffing in Scotland. Snuff-spoons, though, like snuff-mulls, are still produced, and more often with a view to their purchase by collectors of such things than by snuff-takers.

It was a little mull of neat though somewhat neglected appearance—described nearly a century and a quarter ago as 'made of the tip of a horn neatly turned round at the point; with a lid plainly mounted in silver on which is engraven an inscription'—that once caused considerable excitement at a rural auction sale. The occasion was the selling up, in 1825, of the effects of a lately deceased innkeeper, by name Bacon; the auction being held some twelve miles from Dumfries at the roadside posting house that for many years had been Bacon's home. Most of the household furniture and possessions of any importance had been disposed of with difficulty and at low prices to a small and by no means spendthrift gathering of local residents, when the persevering auctioneer invited a bid for the mull. To his considerable astonishment one of the canniest of his audience responded immediately with an offer of a shilling. So extravagant a suggestion was received by the company with an outcry of protest: one man called out, 'It's no' worth twopence!' and several of his friends agreed with him. About to knock the lot down to the only bidder, the auctioneer hesitated long enough to give the tarnished lid of the mull a rub on his coat-sleeve: his first discovery was that of the silver plate, his second that it was inscribed. With some difficulty he was able to decipher the inscription, which, with trembling voice, he read aloud: 'Robert Burns, Officer of the Excise'. There followed in an atmosphere of reverence bids of shilling upon shilling, until, at no less a figure than £5, the mull was declared the property of one of the wealthiest of those present, a Mr. Munnell of Closburn.

Afterwards it was recalled that Bacon, the innkeeper, had been in earlier years a personal friend and boon companion of Burns; that together they had spent many convivial evenings which had inspired not a few of the poet's more festive compositions. The mull, long prized by the posting house master as the gift of his old acquaintance, was passed from hand to hand after its sale at the auction, its new owner inviting each snuff-taker present to try a pinch of its contents. One who availed himself of this offer, and who afterwards related the story of the occasion, spoke highly of the innkeeper's choice of snuff, voting it the 'most pleasant' he had ever sampled.

Snuff-horns, like snuff-boxes, have their table as well as portable forms. The usual table-mull is a single horn mounted at its centre on a solid base of wood or silver.

It may be a fine specimen of a horn with a spectacular curl and measuring a foot or more from end to end: sometimes it will be carved and the small end will be silver-tipped; while its hollowed opposite extremity will be fitted for snuff with a well and hinged lid of silver. On the base may be an inscribed plate recording something of the mull's original ownership, and on the centre of the lid perhaps a little silver statuette of a Highlander, or the figure of a stag or horse, to act as a handle for opening and closing.

The most elaborate of table-mulls, sometimes spoken of as Guild mulls, are those composed of a pair of horns mounted as though upon a head and having a silver snuff-container set between the roots. Some are so impressive in size, decoration and accessories as almost to amount to pieces of furniture. The snuff-container between the outward branching horns may have as many as six compartments, each with a separate lid and handle, for different sorts of snuff, and, attached by silver chains, may be a whole outfit of little implements once made use of by fastidious snuffers. One or two of these instruments will certainly be spoons or nose-shovels; others, a snuff-rake, a small brush and a hare's foot—the last to do duty as a wiper.

The double horns made mulls of this description convenient to pass from hand to hand round a dining-table. Fine examples, particularly, were made for Scottish and other regimental Messes, and in certain regiments they still survive among the older pieces of table plate. One or two continue in use, after dinner going round the table in a clockwise direction with the port. Though appreciation of snuff may be slight compared to what it once was, snuff remains the only form of tobacco that compliments rather than insults good wine.

FINIS

Short Bibliography

Besant, Sir Walter, *London in the Eighteenth Century*, 1902.

—, *London in the Time of the Stuarts*, 1903.

—, *Fifty Years Ago*, 1888.

Billings, E. R., *Tobacco, Its History & Varieties*, Hartford, U.S.A., 1875.

Blondel, S., *Le Tabac*, 1891.

Bragge, William, *Bibliotheca Nicotiana*, 1880.

Connely, Willard, *The Reign of Beau Brummell*, 1940.

Corti, Count, *A History of Smoking*, 1931.

Curtis, Prof. M. M., *The Story of Snuff & Snuff Boxes*, New York, 1935.

Evans, George, *The Old Snuff House of Fribourg & Treyer*, 1921.

Fairholt, F. W., *Tobacco, Its History & Associations*, 1859.

Heal, Sir Ambrose, *The Signboards of Old London Shops*, 1947.

Hone, William, *Everyday Book*, 1826.

—, *Table Book*, 1827.

—, *Year Book*, 1835.

Hunt, Leigh, *The Town*, 1848.

Jesse, William, *The Life of Beau Brummell*, 1844.

Lillie, C., *The French Perfumer*.

Meller, James, *Nicotiana*, 1832.

Norton, R. & M., *A History of Gold Snuff Boxes*, 1938.

Penn, W. A., *The Soverane Herb*, 1901.

Prescott, J., *Tobacco and Its Adulterations*, 1858.

Stemnitz, Andrew, *Smoker's Guide, Philosopher & Friend*, 1877.

Tanner, Edward, *Tobacco from Grower to Smoker*, 4th edn., 1937.

Thompson, C. J. S., *Quacks of Old London*, 1928.

Index